CHILDREN'S WRITER'S
NOTEBOOK

Quarto is the authority on a wide range of topics.

Quarto educates, entertains and enriches the lives of
our readers—enthusiasts and lovers of hands-on living.

www.QuartoKnows.com

Published by Quad Books
Copyright © 2016 Quid Publishing
Conceived, designed and produced by
Quid Publishing
an imprint of The Quarto Group
Level One
Ovest House
58 West Street
Brighton
BN1 2RA
England

ISBN: 978-0-85762-589-2

Printed in China

CHILDREN'S WRITER'S
NOTEBOOK

---

20 Great Authors & 70 Writing Exercises

WES MAGEE

QUAD BOOKS

CONTENTS

DR. SEUSS

BORN: 2 March, 1904
DIED: 24 September, 1991
WRITING: Rhyming fantasy
KEY WORK: *The Cat in the Hat*

Theodor Seuss Geisel (Dr. Seuss) was, and still is, a hugely popular children's author and illustrator. He won the coveted Laura Ingalls Wilder Medal in 1980 for a 'substantial and lasting contribution to children's literature'.

The limited vocabulary book

Born in Springfield, Massachusetts, Dr. Seuss was heavily involved in publishing and advertising before, during and after World War II, as an illustrator, political cartoonist and film animator. In the 1950s he concentrated on writing books for children, and a meeting with William Spaulding, a director with the publisher Houghton Mifflin, brought the issue of books in schools to Seuss's attention. Spaulding felt that reading books for young children were dull and boring. He challenged Seuss to write 'a book that children can't put down', using a limited word list.

On the word list Seuss spotted 'cat' and 'hat'. That simple rhyme was the inspiration for *The Cat in the Hat* (1957). The text he wrote rhymed throughout (it is really a very long poem) and Seuss kept well within the boundaries of William Spaulding's original word list. He thus simplified his previous,

more elaborate writing style. Throughout the 1950s and 1960s, under the pen name Dr. Seuss, he wrote and illustrated a series of books that remain immensely popular worldwide, including classics such as *Henry Hears a Who!* (1955), *How the Grinch Stole Christmas!* (1957), *One Fish Two Fish Red Fish Blue Fish* (1960), *Green Eggs and Ham* (1960), and *Fox in Socks* (1965). They have been adapted as films, TV series and musicals.

Using rhyme and rhythm

Rhyming poetry, with repetition, became Dr. Seuss's forte. It was readily memorised and chanted by young children, who enjoyed the easy familiarity that repeated recitals brought. Seuss favoured simple, one-syllable rhymes. For example, in *The Cat in the Hat* you find: play/day, ball/all and mat/hat. In *One Fish Two Fish Red Fish Blue Fish* there are: star/car/are and run/fun/sun. And *Green Eggs and Ham* features: Sam/

Looking back to his childhood, Dr. Seuss recalled how his mother, Henrietta Seuss Geisel, recited and chanted traditional rhymes at bedtimes, and he later credited her with both his ability and desire to create the rhyming narratives for which he became famous.

Dr. Suess pictured in 1957, working on preparatory drawings for *How the Grinch Stole Christmas*.

> *'The problem with writing a book in verse is, to be successful, it has to sound like you knocked it off on a rainy Friday afternoon. It has to sound easy.'*

– Dr. Seuss

am/ham, box/fox and house/mouse. The verse patterns vary. They can be very short but often lengthen as the story unfolds. In *The Cat in the Hat*, a verse grows to full-page length, as the cat's tricks unfold and the two children watch in amazement.

To create rhythm, Seuss adopted various line lengths and syllable counts. He favoured the 12-syllable line with four beats, which is called anapaestic tetrameter. His delight in the anarchic led him to break poetic rules and change line lengths (and therefore rhythms) within verses. At times the poems are conversation pieces, as in *Green Eggs and Ham*.

Would you like them in a house?
Would you like them with a mouse?

I do not like them in a house.
I do not like them with a mouse.
I do not like them here or there.
I do not like them anywhere.
I do not like green eggs and ham.
I do not like them Sam-I-Am.

The questioning character's (Sam-I-Am) lines have seven syllables, while the response lines have eight syllables. This gives a slight rhythm change within the conversation.

Cartoonish, surreal illustrations

Dr. Seuss's illustrations relate closely to the text. The young child, as listener or as independent reader, easily identifies what's happening in the pictures. Seuss used black outlines, often with black line shading, and two colours. In his books, the large text is set out on the left-hand page and given plenty of white space within which to breathe. The illustrations appear on the opposite page: a close correlation between reading and looking.

001

Rhyming words

Dr. Seuss's use of simple, one-syllable rhyming words is a key element in his texts.

Exercise: Write a rhyming word list about, say, a child's bedroom at night. The rhymes should use single-syllable words, such as 'door'/'floor', 'red'/'bed' and 'light'/'night'. A rhyming dictionary will help.

Now introduce a blue mouse in the house. Write rhyming couplets listing all the things the mouse could do at night in the child's bedroom. The couplet lines should have eight and nine syllables.

The blue Mouse in the House then said,
as the small Child sat up in her bed,
'Watch me run up the squeaky door,
and watch me slide on the wooden floor'.

The zanier the mouse's actions, the better. Come up with a surprise ending.

#002

Experimenting with running-on rhyme

Dr. Seuss books typically feature rhyming couplets. Can you make the rhyming words run on and on (and on)?

Choose a single-syllable word, such as 'door', and make a list of all the words that rhyme with it, including words with more than one syllable, such as 'explore' and 'encore'.

Exercise: Now write a nonsense verse that runs on for as long as possible. For example:

Jasper the dog pushed open the door,
he walked in and began to explore,
then skated along the polished floor.

003

Rhyming verse

An extract from _The Cat in the Hat_:

'Now! Now! Have no fear.
Have no fear!' said the cat.
'My tricks are not bad,'
Said the Cat in the Hat.

Exercise: Write about a dog doing silly things on its walk. Draft a verse similar to Dr. Seuss's example: four lines with a rhyme scheme A, B, C, B. Make the syllable count in the four lines: 5, 6, 5, 6.

The wordcount is small, so you can easily redraft a number of times to achieve a good, rhythmic result. Keep the subject matter nonsensical.

Having achieved a single verse, compose further verses, recounting what happens on the dog's walk. Make use of repetition.

MARGARET WISE BROWN

BORN: 23 May, 1910
DIED: 13 November, 1952
WRITING: Picture books for the very young
KEY WORK: *Goodnight Moon*

Margaret Wise Brown was a prolific writer of book texts for the very young. Her easy-flowing, poetic writing, allied with illustrations from the likes of Leonard Weisgard and Clement Hurd, created hugely popular picture books.

Soothing author, restless person

Despite her tragic early death at the age of 42, Wise Brown produced many books, the first of which was *When the Wind Blew* (1937). She also wrote under various pseudonyms, including Golden MacDonald, Kainbuck Brown and Juniper Sage. Her books sold in their millions, and two of them, *Little Lost Lamb* and *The Little Island*, won the Caldecott Medal in 1947. Among her best-known books are *The Runaway Bunny* (1942), *The Little Island* (1946), *Goodnight Moon* (1947) and *Big Red Barn* (1954).

In terms of language, structure and subject matter, Brown's writing style is deceptively simple. Beneath the simplicity is a truly poetic talent. While the words on the page appear to be easily achieved, they are filled with an emotional quality to which children readily respond.

Animals feature widely in the books. They represent the child who hears the bedtime story, as in *Goodnight Moon*, where a small rabbit is preparing to go to sleep in 'the great green room'. Many items in the room are listed – telephone, red balloon, picture on the wall and so on. There are kittens and a 'quiet old lady' (mummy rabbit). The small rabbit falls asleep to the lulling effect of 'goodnight' repetitions ('goodnight clocks/ And goodnight socks'). There is rhyme and the rhythm is lulling, but punctuation is absent. It all looks rather like an early draft of a bedtime poem, yet even this seeming early draft is powerfully effective. It certainly caught the attention of the American nation.

Unusual method

Throughout her life, the author wrote down fragments of ideas, feelings, observations and rhythmic combinations of words that appealed to her, and then worked to create loosely structured poems or rhythmic prose.

While a student at Hollins College, Wise Brown was encouraged to write by her literature professor, Marguerite Hearsey. In her first published book, *When the Wind Blew* (1937), Wise Brown inscribed a copy to Hearsey with the words '...and always thanking you for the first encouragement'.

Hollins University, Virginia, where Wise Brown studied English. She graduated in 1932.

She often eschewed punctuation, as it got in the way of the unfolding narrative.

She loved animals and this is reflected in her books, in which characters are often small creatures. Oddly, however, in a profile published in *Life* magazine, when the reporter expressed surprise that the author of rabbit-themed books didn't mind at all about hunting and shooting rabbits, she replied, 'Well, I don't especially like children either, at least, not as a group'.

Brown also collaborated closely with the artists who provided the pictures. A notable example is *Goodnight Moon*, in which Clement Hurd's beautifully judged shaded drawings and full-colour double-page paintings match the bedtime poem perfectly. There are echoes of well-known nursery rhymes within the sparse text. The final spread shows everything listed in the book's text, plus an illustration of the young rabbit safely asleep in his comfortable bed. 'Goodnight noises everywhere' is the complete text on the final spread, notably lacking a period. It creates the feeling of bedtime peace and quiet.

Using key attributes

Brown possessed an almost childlike way of observing the world. This is clearly discernible in *The Important Book* (1949), in which she lists what is important about various things that a child would commonly know about – the Sun, the Moon, wind, rain, a pencil, insects. Take for example, 'The important thing about rain is that it is wet'. The same two lines are repeated at the end. Brown called these the 'key attributes'. In between is a list of things about rain.

'Quietness is an essential part of all awareness. In quiet times and sleepy times, a child can dwell in thoughts of his own, and in songs and stories of his own.'

— Margaret Wise Brown

Creatures and their actions

Brown kept her books simple, subject-wise and vocabulary-wise. She used repetitions and echoes of words used earlier in the book.

Exercise: Compose a verse in similar style. The subject matter could be a kind of weather (snow, hail, thunder) or items in a garden (flowers, trees, pond). Beginning with an observable statement, compose a further five lines, giving simple facts about the subject. Repeat the opening lines at the end. Make use of 'accidental' rhyme.

Poetic lists

Exercise: Choose a pet, such as a dog, cat, hamster or rabbit. List things the pet does, keeping the activities simple. Make some lines longer and add rhymes here and there. For instance:

The cat sleeps

it runs

it purrs quietly

Now divide the 'poetic list' up, with each line in its own space (as though on an individual page).

Hide and seek

The Runaway Bunny is one of Margaret Wise Brown's classic picture books for the very young. It tells the tale of a baby rabbit who repeatedly runs away, and the mother rabbit who always brings him home. The author uses repetition to give the story continuity.

Exercise: Write a simple text for a picture book about two creatures (a young one and its mother) who are playing hide and seek. The creatures can be domesticated or wild. The young creature hides in various places, while the mother keeps on searching. A refrain could be, 'And I will find you'.

MAURICE SENDAK

BORN: 10 June, 1928
DIED: 8 May, 2012
WRITING: Picture books
KEY WORK: *Where the Wild Things Are*

Following a troubled childhood, Maurice Sendak rose to prominence as a picture book author and artist, gaining international acclaim for the iconic Where the Wild Things Are, *which was published in 1963.*

A troubled background

As the child of Jewish immigrants in New York, some of whose Polish relatives had been killed in the Holocaust, Maurice Sendak grew up in an unsettling atmosphere of depression and anger. It was seeing the Walt Disney film *Fantasia* at the age of 12 that gave him the desire to draw and illustrate. During his youth, he sketched caricatures of the immigrant relatives who regularly turned up at the Sendak's Brooklyn home. He described them as 'All crazy..... crazy faces and wild eyes.....with big yellow teeth.....unkempt, and hair unravelling out of their noses'. Later on, those drawings became the basis for the unnamed monsters depicted in *Where the Wild Things Are.*

In the 1950s, Maurice Sendak illustrated books written by his brother, Jack Sendak, before branching out on his own to create picture books that had an edge to them – he

described his work as having 'no sunshine or rainbows, because that's not real life'. He began working closely with Ursula Nordstrom, a director at Harper Row publishers, who became a pivotal figure in his rise to fame.

Fiercely successful

Where the Wild Things Are is seen as a watershed book in the world of picture books. When it was published, the book, with its pictures of horned, fanged, grotesque monsters, proved controversial, and concerns were raised among parents that it would frighten children. To young readers today, the monsters appear benign and smiling, but in 1963 the book was edgy and subversive.

The story begins with a boy's anger. Max pulls on his wolf suit, rebels, and is sent to bed without any supper. Thereafter he sets out on a dreamlike (perhaps nightmarish)

During Sendak's troubled early years, he was deeply affected by the infamous kidnap and eventual murder of Charles Lindbergh Jr. in 1932. At the time the event prompted a media frenzy. Despite being only three years old, Sendak said he vividly remembered the tragedy.

Sendak photographed at his home in Ridgefield, Connecticut, in 1990.

journey to the land where the wilds things live. He returns to his bedroom to find his supper there on a tray.

The text is spare, containing a mere 338 words. It is honed to contain only essential information, without any padding. Some sentences roll on from page to page to page. The text is clearly laid out (against a white background) at the bottom of the illustrated pages and relates directly to the pictures. There are textual echoes, such as Max's mother calling him a 'wild thing' and the boy responding with 'I'll eat you up', both of which are repeated in the land of the wild things.

The illustrations, with their subdued colours, black-line shadings, and cross-hatching, are sumptuous. At the centre of the book are three fully illustrated double-page spreads, without any text.

After the wild things

Sendak invited further criticism when *In the Night Kitchen* was published in 1970. It featured drawings of a naked boy prancing through the story. The nudity was too much for some, and the book was censored in a

'[Sendak was] unique, grumpy, brilliant, gay, wise, magical and made the world better by creating art in it.'

– Author Neil Gaiman

number of American states. When *Outside Over There* (1981) was published, it combined with the earlier books to create a trilogy of titles about childhood. *Where the Wild Things Are* focused on early childhood, *In the Night Kitchen* on boyhood, and *Outside Over There* on pre-adolescence. In the three books, Sendak showed children coping with feelings of anger, danger, boredom and fear, and how they learn to master such feelings.

The author continued to produce high-quality, richly illustrated books until his death in 2012, at the age of 83. The stories were animated for TV series in the 1970s.

Kooky characters

Sendak got the idea for his characters from the eccentric cast of relatives that used to visit his family home.

Exercise: Write descriptions of three or four people you know. They could be family members, a teacher from school, someone you worked with or a person you once met. Concentrate on the characteristics and mannerisms you think are odd, or could be made to appear odd. Write one paragraph for each person.

Now work on the descriptions, so that they bind together to make a 'family' or 'group'. They could form the basis for a story.

Good and bad at bedtime

After a long day, children can sometimes be docile, able to do something quiet and positive before going to bed. Alternatively, if overtired, they may get up to all manner of mischief. Both scenarios provide fodder for writers' imaginations.

Exercise: In the two columns below, list ten examples of good and bad bedtime behaviour. Draw on your own childhood memories and knowledge of children.

Good bedtime behaviour	Bad bedtime behaviour

#009

Rumpus

'Let the wild rumpus start!' was Max's order to the wild things in *Where the Wild Things Are*. Sendak depicted the rumpus in three fully illustrated double-page spreads. He didn't use a single word.

Exercise: Try to imagine what Max and the monsters did at the 'wild rumpus'. Write a 300-word description of all the wonderful, wacky and wild things they get up to. Make plentiful use of noises and short phrases, such as 'Arrgghh', 'Eeeeeee', 'Watch out!' and 'Go!'

#010

A picture-book story

Picture books often contain few words and can be very thin, with fewer than 40 pages. They tell their story with minimal text. _Where the Wild Things Are_, for example, has only 338 words.

Exercise: Draft a short story of 250 words. Using _Where the Wild Things Are_ as an example, send one character (a boy or girl) on a journey. Leaving the house, they could go, say, through the woods, to an island or even out into space. Who, or what, does the child encounter? What happens? The child returns home safely after the adventure.

Now redraft your story until it is tight. No padding. Using extra paper, make a mock-up of a 24-page book and write your story out. Make sure that each page ends with something significant, so that the reader will want to turn the page to find out what happens next. Give your book a title, one that works as a 'door' into the story. You can, if you like, add illustrations.

JEAN DE BRUNHOFF

BORN: 6 December, 1899
DIED: 16 October, 1937
WRITING: Fantasy picture books
KEY WORK: *The Story of Babar*

Born in Paris, France, Jean de Brunhoff was a painter who wrote and illustrated a series of classic picture books about Babar the Elephant. Maurice Sendak described de Brunhoff as 'a master of the picture book form'.

Bedtime storytelling

Cecile, Jean de Brunhoff's wife, dreamed up a story about a small elephant that leaves the jungle to come and live in a city as a bedtime story for her two young sons. The boys asked their father (an accomplished professional painter) to draw pictures for the story. Jean de Brunhoff wrote a text and drew and painted pictures, so creating Babar the Elephant. The first book, *The Story of Babar, the Little Elephant* was published by Editions du Jardin des Modes, which specialised in fashion.

Jean de Brunhoff died prematurely (aged 37), having finished five Babar picture books. His son, Laurent, completed the remaining two to make a series of seven books. Thereafter Laurent continued to write and illustrate Babar books, closely following his late father's style.

An illustrated masterpiece

The illustrations in *Babar the Elephant* are painterly and beautifully composed. They have a charm that beguiles the young reader. Jean de Brunhoff's original texts were printed in cursive writing, which made the books look as though they had been handwritten. The text is straightforward yet poetic, and it has a charming quality.

The Story of Babar launched the series in 1931. It appeared as an oversized volume and was an immediate publishing success. The six books that followed recount episodes in Babar's life, as he rises from being a small orphaned elephant to become king of the elephants. Upon arriving in a big city, he acquires a smart green suit, adopts the customs of western society and becomes fully civilised. Eventually, he returns to his homeland and is a civilising influence on the other elephants.

In an interview with Laurent de Brunhoff, the son who continued to create Barbar books after his father's untimely death, the interviewer mentioned that 'General Charles de Gaulle famously said he liked the Barbar books so much because Babar the elephant gives 'a certain idea of France'.

An illustration from *Zephyr's Holidays* by Jean de Brunhoff, published in 1936.

In contrast to the softly stunning watercolours and line drawings, the stories include a number of traumatic events. For example, early in the first book, Babar's mother is shot by a hunter. Yet this becomes subsumed in the warm, comforting tone of the deliberately naive stories.

The books received international acclaim and remain popular picture books to this day. Their appeal is broad, and they are appreciated by adults as well as children. In his introduction to the English edition of *The Travels of Babar*, A. A. Milne wrote, 'If you love elephants, you will love Babar and Celeste. If you are grown-up and have never been fascinated by a picture book before, then this is the one that will fascinate you.'

'The Babar stories, ranked with the Beatrix Potter books, are the best ever made for very young children.'

– Roger Sale, in *Fairy Tales and After: From Snow White to E. B. White.*

Interpretation and controversy

As the decades have passed and social attitudes have changed, the Babar books have been criticised. Accusations of imperialism, colonialism and racism have been laid at the author's door. Some felt children were being given the message that the life of an elephant in the wild could be dangerous and painful, and it was therefore safer to be an elephant in a city house near a park.

The elephant was seen as a native African arriving naked in a civilised imperial capital city, where he quickly acquired the 'superior' dress and habits of western society. On his return to his homeland, Babar persuades the other elephants to adopt his 'superior' habits, and then goes on to defeat the warlike rhinoceroses, who refuse to accept this conditioning.

These are of course adult interpretations of the stories. Children are free to enjoy the books' magical, imaginative qualities.

A royal return

After his time in the city, Babar returns home and is crowned king.

Exercise: Draw up a list of the new king's commandments – an imaginative (and even outrageous) list, to delight and entrance young readers. Include other animals (lions, snakes, ostriches, camels, monkeys, parrots – they all appear in the Babar books) in the commandments.

Reversing roles

The animal that comes to live in a human environment is a common theme in stories. Like other creatures before him, Babar is amazed when he reaches the town ('What strange things he saw!').

Exercise: Reverse the situation and describe what a human child would think and feel about going to live in a tropical rainforest, such as the Amazon. Compose six or seven short paragraphs, mentioning the sights, sounds, weather, and his or her encounters with creatures, and conclude with a happy outcome.

A strange environment

Babar the Elephant leaves 'the Great Forest' and takes up residence in a city. This premise gave Jean de Brunhoff plenty of contrasting material to play with, as Babar came to terms with his new, and alien, surroundings.

Exercise: Draft a 300-word story for very young children about a young creature (for example, a crocodile, panda or polar bear) who is transported to the moon. How does the young creature adapt to his or her new life and surroundings? What does he or she do? Who, or what, does he or she meet? As the story ends, the young creature returns to planet Earth none the worse for his adventures. Be sure that the language you use is age-appropriate.

Use the space below to collect your thoughts. Once you have the outline, organise the story into segments, as you would find in a picture book.

A. A. MILNE

BORN: 18 January, 1882
DIED: 31 January, 1958
WRITING: Fantasy; poetry
KEY WORK: *Winnie-the-Pooh*

Primarily an English playwright and novelist, Alan Alexander Milne gained international fame in the 1920s when he published poems and stories for children based on his infant son's (Christopher Robin) pastimes and soft toys.

Family inspiration

In the early 20th century, Alan Alexander Milne was the archetypal English author: a privately educated Cambridge University graduate and successful literary gentleman around London town. At university he edited the student periodical *Granta*, contributed humorous verse to *Punch* and went on to be a prolific writer of plays and novels. His Sussex country house, Cotchford Farm, bordered upon Ashdown Forest in the southeast of England.

In 1920, the birth of his son, Christopher Robin Milne, proved a fresh source of inspiration. Milne wrote rhyming verse based on observations of his infant son's activities and collection of soft toys, especially a teddy bear called Edward. Subsequently, a book of children's verse, *When We Were Very Young*, was published in 1924. The poems proved extremely popular and entered the British national consciousness. They were a mix of extended narratives ('The King's Breakfast'), first-person musings ('Brownie', 'The Island' and 'Halfway Down') and verses about invented characters ('Mary Jane', 'Alice' and 'Dormouse'). A second collection, *Now We Are Six*, followed in 1927. It included such famous rhyming poems as 'The Little Black Hen', 'Forgiven' and 'Furry Bear'. Milne extended this interest into fiction. The enduring *Winnie-the-Pooh* (1926) and *House at Pooh Corner* (1928) featured not only Christopher Robin but also the boy's

---

'The only excuse which I have discovered for writing anything is that I want to write it.'

– A. A. Milne

Milne enlisted in the British Army and served in France during World War I. Following repatriation due to illness, his writing skills were put to use when he was recruited into a secret propaganda unit, M17b. Many years later, in 1934 he published a denunciation of war, *Peace with Honour*.

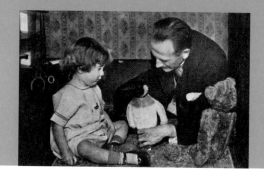

Milne with his son Christopher, playing with the toys that inspired the Pooh characters.

soft toys: Winnie-the-Pooh, 'the bear of very little brain'; Piglet; Eeyore; Kanga; Roo; and Tigger.

The poems

The poems have undoubted charm and now seem indelibly set in time. They describe a whimsical world of the nanny, the nursery and solitary games. Milne proved a wonderfully inventive master of rhyme and rhythm, and he often employed wordplay and humor. Every poem in the two collections for children is different. He took intense care with composition and layout, giving the poems a shaped, painterly look. A fellow contributor to British satirical magazine *Punch*, H. E. Shepard provided sketchy line drawings for the books, and the combination of Milne and Shepard proved irresistible to the book-buying public. The readers adored the image of an idyllic childhood complete with beloved playthings.

The stories

Told by a narrator, *Winnie-the-Pooh* is related as a series of adventures set in 100-Acre Wood, based on Ashdown Forest, which bordered the Milnes' house. Each chapter has a précis heading, and there are rhymes and minipoems throughout. He incorporated wordplay and gentle humor. The author's unique voice is intimate: he addresses the readers as if they are friends. He suspends disbelief by drawing the reader – child or adult – completely into the tales. The tone is warm and comfortable. One by one, the other characters are introduced, and each chapter is an adventure story in its own right.

Succinct dialogue

Milne used dialogue to propel the action forwards and inform the reader about the characters' personalities. Take this example, which shows how Milne was able to communicate feelings:

> 'Is this it?' said Eeyore, a little surprised.
> Piglet nodded.
> 'My present?'
> Piglet nodded again.
> 'The balloon?'
> 'Yes.'
> 'Thank you, Piglet', said Eeyore. 'You don't mind my asking', he went on, 'but what colour was this balloon when it – when it was a balloon?'
> 'Red.'

Inventing characters from your childhood

A. A. Milne drew inspiration for his characters from observing his infant son playing with his toys. Think back to your own childhood. Can you recall any favourite (or indeed hated) toys? They could be soft toys, such as teddy bears, gremlins, snakes, rag dolls and dogs, or something mechanical like a train, a bus or model cars.

Exercise: Make a list of five childhood toys. Give each toy a new name – for example, a cuddly dog could be called Hugbug. Now write a brief description of each newly named toy, so that they become familiar as characters. Choose a setting that you know well, such as a beach, a field or a garden. Write a chapter of around 300 words, describing the newly named characters' adventures.

#015

Amusing dialogue

As we have seen, A. A. Milne gave life to his characters through lively and often amusing dialogue.

Exercise: Select two of the characters you created in the previous exercise. Create a dialogue between them. It could be an exchange about something they found or lost. Bring in the feelings that the characters experience, and try to keep the conversation consistent with the two characters. Can you add the ingredient of light humor? Bring the conversation to an end with a single word.

#016

The game

In Milne's fiction, the game Poohsticks played by Christopher Robin involves standing on a wooden bridge, dropping twigs into a stream, and waiting to see which one reaches the other side of the bridge first. It has become part of the lore of many a childhood.

Exercise: Invent a new game to be played by soft toy characters in a children's story. It could be something like throwing handfuls of cut grass or walking along a fallen tree trunk, making daisy chains or jumping across puddles. Create a scene where one character explains the rules. Then describe them playing the game. How does the game end?

#017

Using maps

Maps can play a significant role in books for children. The map in Robert Louis Stevenson's *Treasure Island* is central, and in *The House at Pooh Corner* there's a map of 100-Acre Wood, showing where the various characters live – for example, 'Piglets House' – and interesting and amusing labels, such as 'Floody Place' and 'To North Pole'.

Exercise: Design a map for a book, as drawn and labelled by a story character who is a poor speller. Label places and interesting features. Draw compass points and add signposts to distant places.

ANTOINE DE SAINT-EXUPÉRY

BORN: 29 June, 1900
DIED: 31 July, 1944
WRITING: Fantasy fable
KEY WORK: *The Little Prince*

A French writer and aviator, Antoine de Saint-Exupéry wrote not only award-winning, philosophical books for adults, but also a book for children, The Little Prince. *A fantasy fable, it became one of the world's most translated books.*

A crash in the desert

Like Roald Dahl (see pages 58–59), Antoine de Saint-Exupéry suffered a dramatic and traumatic event, when the aeroplane he was piloting crashed in the desert. Just as Dahl used that experience in his early writings, so Saint-Exupéry drew on the experience to create an iconic novella for children, *The Little Prince.*

Saint-Exupéry was an experienced commercial pilot who wrote lyrically about his flying experiences, notably in the book *Night Flight* (1931). He joined the Free French air force during World War II and was known to daringly read and write during his solo flights. Upon demobilisation, he went to the USA, where he published books for adults and was persuaded by his publisher to write a book for children. It took over two years, but eventually *The Little Prince* appeared in the USA in 1943. It wasn't released in France until 1945.

Antoine de Saint-Exupéry's life had a tragic end: he disappeared on a solo flight on July 31, 1944. It is thought he crashed into the Mediterranean Sea.

The Little Prince

The Little Prince story is a fantasy fable with charmingly naive watercolour illustrations by the author. The 28 short chapters are narrated six years after the event ('I have never yet told this story') by a pilot who crash-landed in the Sahara desert. While attempting to repair the plane ('more isolated than a shipwrecked sailor on a raft in the middle of the ocean'), he is visited by a small, elegantly costumed person with golden hair, who had fallen to Earth from a tiny asteroid. The narrator names his strange visitor 'the little prince'.

The pilot narrator writes about his conversations with the visitor, recounting the story told to him about the little prince's tiny

In the late 1920s, Saint-Exupéry's varied aviation experience saw him appointed as director of a remote airfield in the Sahara region of southern Morocco. Here he developed a love for the desert, living a secluded existence in a ramshackle wooden abode, where he slept on a thin straw mattress.

Antoine de Saint-Exupéry pictured with his wife Consuelo in their Paris apartment in 1936.

asteroid home, with its three minuscule volcanoes, baobab tree and rose flower. The tale of the prince's space travels, and his encounters with numerous characters, are all illuminated by Exupéry's illustrations. The story ends with the prince's mystical disappearance: 'There was nothing there but a flash of yellow close to the ankle [...] He fell as gently as a tree falls. There was not even any sound, because of the sand.'

The book has proved immensely popular. It has been translated numerous times and adapted for stage and screen.

> *'Rarely have an author and a character been so intimately bound as Antoine de Saint-Exupéry and his Little Prince. [...] The two remain tangled together, twin innocents who fell from the sky.'*
>
> – Stacy Schiff, *The New York Times*

The style

The story is an adult fable presented as a children's book and told in a measured tone, as the stranded pilot recounts the prince's story. It includes many observations about the nature of life on Earth, including social criticism and philosophical conversations, the latter with a fox the little prince encounters: '"Men have forgotten the truth", said the fox. "But you must not forget it. You become responsible, forever, for what you have tamed."'

The book's brief chapters are written in short, direct sentences, with plenty of dialogue. Indeed, some chapters are almost entirely dialogue, with the narrator combining these with only short interjectory paragraphs of commentary.

Themes emerge in the writing: loneliness, sadness, even despair, and ultimately triumph. These qualities give the book a muted tone, yet the reader is constantly drawn forwards into other imagined worlds by the author's unforced, easy style.

018

An alien on Earth

The little prince, elegantly costumed, falls to Earth from a tiny asteroid. Reality, and the laws of science that govern it, are suspended by the author as he recounts the tale. Adults may baulk at this lack of realism, but children aren't concerned by the unreality of such fantastical space travel. They feel that anything is possible.

Exercise 1: Write a passage (three or four paragraphs) describing an alien coming to planet Earth. Let the alien meet a person or creature. This is not a new concept: it is the basis for a number of stories and films, but the idea still has plenty of unused mileage.

_____

_____

_____

_____

_____

_____

_____

Now rewrite the passage, converting the description into conversation, as Antoine de Saint-Exupéry did so expertly in *The Little Prince*. Begin with a brief introduction, then let the conversation between the alien and the person or creature it meets take place. Keep the questions and the responses short and to the point. Give the conversation a philosophical slant or tone.

_____

_____

_____

_____

_____

_____

_____

_____

_____

_____

_____

_____

_____

_____

_____

_____

#019

When I was six: a memoir

The pilot's narration in *The Little Prince* begins with something he remembered reading in a book as a six-year-old:

'Boa constrictors swallow their prey whole, without chewing it. After that they are not able to move, and they sleep through the six months that they need for digestion.'

Exercise: Try to recall something you read or saw in a book when you were young. Drawing upon that distant memory, see if you can dredge up details. Where were you? When? Was anyone with you at that time? Can you recall the feel of the paper or book? Was there a certain smell that you associate with that moment? What was in the book? Write a 100-word memoir piece recalling this moment.

#020

An account of a new planet

Before falling to Earth, the little prince had previously visited six strange planets, and he is eager to share his stories with the pilot.

Exercise: Write an account of a seventh planet visited by the little prince. The planet will be small, it will have two or three remarkable features and its sole inhabitant will be a person noteworthy for something he or she has invented. Use dialogue to move the account forwards.

ROALD DAHL

BORN: 13 September, 1916
DIED: 23 November, 1990
WRITING: Adventure; fantasy
KEY WORK: *Charlie and the Chocolate Factory*

'One of the greatest storytellers for children of the 20th century' is how Roald Dahl has been described. He was a novelist, poet and screenwriter whose books have been adapted as films and stage plays, and which remain popular today.

Another crash in the desert

While a World War II fighter pilot with the RAF, Roald Dahl crashed in the Libyan desert and sustained multiple injuries. After convalescing, he was posted to the British Embassy in Washington, D.C., where he helped promote British interests in the USA. There he encountered a similarly employed author, C. S. Forester, who was writing adventure stories for his Captain Horatio Hornblower series. Forester encouraged Dahl to write about his wartime exploits, and in August 1942 his first published work, *Shot down over Libya*, appeared in *The Saturday Evening Post*.

A passage from that first piece sign-posted Dahl's style: direct, swiftly paced and unfussy: 'Shorty carefully extracted a fly from his tea and flicked it across the room. Then he read it [the military order] for a second time. 'Hell's bells, what a piece of cake! Shall I take my flight, sir? We'll have to start right away!" The piece also indicated what was to become Dahl's fascination with characters' names.

The books begin

Although *The Gremlins*, a story based on his experiences as a fighter pilot, was published by Walt Disney and Random House in the USA in 1943, it wasn't until 1961 that his first genuine children's book appeared. *James and the Giant Peach* proved to be the start of a long run of highly successful stories that included *The Witches*, *Matilda*, *Charlie and the Chocolate Factory* and *George's Marvellous Medicine*, until his last book, *The Minpins*, was published in 1991. Some have been filmed and dramatised.

Roald Dahl's writing is unsentimental, darkly comic, macabre, and the stories often have surprise endings. Characteristically, he often wrote from a child character's point of view. Adults were mostly 'bad' and depicted as

In an interview, Felicity Dahl, Roald's second wife, tells how he used to get grumpy when he was finishing a book. 'I remember saying, "But you should be pleased when you're reaching the end". And he used to say, "You don't understand – it's the fear of never writing another one!"'

Roald Dahl's favoured writing place was a shed in the garden of his home, Gypsy House.

villainous and physically unattractive people who disliked, loathed or mistreated children. The 'good' young overcome adversity in the end. The book critic Amanda Craig stated, 'He was unequivocal that it is the good, young and kind who triumph over the old, greedy and wicked'.

Characters, and their names
Roald Dahl's inventiveness with his characters' names meant they were instantly memorable and endeared themselves (even the vile ones) to young readers. They include Willy Wonka, Bruce Bogtrotter, Augustus Gloop, Miss Agatha Trunchbull, Matilda Wormwood and Veruca Salt, among many others. The three thoroughly nasty farmers in *Fantastic Mr. Fox* typify many of the adult characters in Dahl's stories. Boggis is enormously fat, gluttonous and dim-witted; Bunce is pot-bellied and dwarf-like; and Bean is lanky, skinny and addicted to strong cider.

A number of illustrators had featured in Dahl's books, but it was with the publication of *The Enormous Crocodile* in 1977 that Quentin Blake's spidery, sketchy pictures made their first appearance. Thereafter, Quentin Blake became synonymous with Dahl's books and the pair worked in tandem until the author's death in 1990.

Verse, mostly in rhyming couplets, was never far away from a Dahl book. Not only did he write books of poetry (*Revolting Rhymes*, 1982, and *Dirty Beasts*, 1984) but also included lengthy narrative poems in the stories. In *Revolting Rhymes* Dahl reinterprets fairy stories, giving them a surprise twist at the end. A rhyming couplet from *Little Red Riding Hood and the Wolf* demonstrates Dahl's directness and his penchant for being outrageous and rude:

> *The small girl smiles. One eyelid flickers.*
> *She whips a pistol from her knickers.*

'Books shouldn't be daunting, they should be funny, exciting and wonderful.'
– **Roald Dahl**

021

Naming characters

Characters' names are pivotal in Roald Dahl stories. As well as those mentioned in the profile on pages 58–59, other Dahl creations include Mike Teavee, the BFG, Lavender, the Twits, Violet Beauregarde, Charlie Bucket, the Oompa-Loompas and Muggle-Wump.

Exercise: Put an unusual first name (it could be old-fashioned, for example) with a surname that is a condiment or a sauce – for example, Albert Tomato-Ketchup or Phyllis 'Sneezer' Pepper. Draw up a list of five or more such names.

Choose the one that works best and compose a character sketch in a single paragraph, describing his or her looks, clothing, hair, facial expressions, peculiarities and habits.

#022

A conference speech

Roald Dahl's story *The Witches* features a convention of witches, all in disguise, which is held in the ballroom of a hotel. The hero manages to sneak in and hears the chief witch's speech.

Exercise: Compose a script for a speech to be delivered by an evil wizard to a conference of newly qualified wizards and their assistants. It should contain welcoming remarks (name the wizard), an explanation of what being an evil wizard entails, a chilling anecdote, advice on who to be wary of in one's wizardly duties and warnings about less-than-thoroughly-evil behaviour. It should end with the speaker wishing the wizards extremely evil spells.

#023

Outlandish recipes

In *Revolting Recipes* Roald Dahl demonstrated yet another facet of his imagination: he concocted amazing dishes. In *Charlie and the Chocolate Factory* he outlined the recipe for Scrumptious Fudgemallow Delight, while in *The BFG* he tells the reader all about Frobscottle, a fizzy drink in which the bubbles go down rather than up.

Exercise: Dream up a new, amazingly delicious (or disgusting) food or dish, especially suitable for children. Name the food, list the ingredients and then add brief notes on the preparation and cooking.

Name of dish:

Ingredients:	Preparation and cooking:

Ingredients: **Preparation and cooking:**

024

Going the whole hog

In *Matilda*, the eponymous heroine says, 'Never do anything by halves if you want to get away with it. Be outrageous. Go the whole hog'. It could well be an appropriate motto for Roald Dahl's writing. He would dream up an idea for a story. Then stretch it. Then go further still.

Exercise: Write a short story (in 250 words) in which a child has to confront two nasty adults who have unpleasant habits. The story could be set, for example, in a school or a hotel, or at a sports event. Let the child be the narrator, and write in the first-person.

Keep the sentences short and to the point, try to bring in humor and add a surprise ending.

HANS CHRISTIAN ANDERSEN

BORN: 2 April, 1805
DIED: 4 August, 1875
WRITING: Fairy stories
KEY WORK: *Fairy Tales*

Best known for his collections of original fairy stories, Hans Christian Andersen was also a prolific writer of novels, plays, poems and travelogues. His books of new fairy tales were widely translated and became internationally popular.

Starting with traditional tales

Initially, Andersen's fairy stories were retellings of old tales from his childhood. Later, he started to create original tales, and eventually *Fairy Tales* was published in two volumes in 1835 and 1837. They included work that was to become famous across the world, stories such as *The Tinder-Box*, *Thumbelina*, *The Little Mermaid* and *The Emperor's New Clothes*.

Initially the books were poorly received. It wasn't until 1845, when the volumes were translated, that interest was aroused. Andersen continued to write fairy stories, and collections were published until 1873. In all, he created 168 original fairy tales.

Belatedly he gained full recognition in his homeland for his innovative and influential work. His image appeared on Danish postage stamps, he was awarded a government stipend as 'a national treasure'

and the Hans Christian Andersen Award was established. Statues of Andersen abound in Denmark and around the world. His stories have been repeatedly adapted as films, musicals and TV shows.

Technique

Andersen's key technique was to make inanimate objects, such as toys, come to life, and to give creatures the power of speech. It was a ploy used later by the likes of Lewis Carroll and Beatrix Potter. He laid the foundations for *Winnie-the-Pooh*.

The stories contain non-didactic moral messages, conveyed through fantasy and humor. Unlike the Brothers Grimm, who ferreted out and drew together Germanic folk tales that had been present in oral culture for centuries, Andersen created his stories from scratch. While he knew the traditional tales well, he gave the genre a thorough reworking.

Andersen first visited England in 1847 and met the British author Charles Dickens, with whom he formed a close friendship. The two writers found common ground in their depictions of the poor. A later, 'brief' visit turned into a five week stay, with Andersen eventually being told to leave.

A painting of Hans Christian Andersen's *The Snow Queen*, by Elena Ringo.

> *'It was when he delved into his own psyche to create his unforgettable cast of tin soldiers, matchgirls and mermaids that his work took on a new dimension.'*

– **Paul Binding, reviewing in *The Guardian***

Andersen said, 'The whole world is a series of miracles, but we're so used to them we call them ordinary things'. He imbued the 'ordinary' with magic.

The fairy tales

Beginning with *The Tinder-Box* in 1835 and ending with *The Flea and the Professor* in 1873, Hans Christian Andersen wrote fairy tales that were often lengthy – many are long enough as to be considered children's books in their own right. He also wrote in long sentences, often using colons and commas to extend the exposition. *The Little Mermaid* (1836) begins, 'Far out in the ocean, where the water is as blue as the prettiest cornflower, and as clear as crystal, it is very, very deep, so deep indeed that no cable could fathom it.'

Andersen's writing is quiet, rather like a soothing murmur in the reader's ear. There is a sense that he is speaking directly to you in a gentle, unhurried manner, and he's about to impart something private and personal (and even secret). It is the voice of a born storyteller. Sometimes he began a new tale in the most traditional way, as in *The Wicked Prince* (1840): 'There lived once upon a time a wicked prince whose heart and mind were set upon conquering all the countries in the world, and on frightening people'. It is yet another example of Andersen's unmistakeable voice, drawing the reader into the narrative that is about to unfold at its own unhurried pace.

Translation can often alter an author's tone, yet Andersen's work comes off the page as fresh as the day it was written. The characters he created are innumerable: the reader is presented with a vast canvas crowded with hobgoblins, witches, soldiers, princesses, swineherds and emperors.

025

Once upon a time

'Once upon a time' is the traditional way of beginning a fairytale, denoting that the tale takes place in the distant past and indicating that the storyteller is about to set out his or her narrative.

Exercise: Create four characters, using the following prompts:

- An older person who needs help
- An innocent yet good person
- A bad, evil or wicked person
- A creature

Introduce a magical element (an object, spell or potion). The setting is a journey (it could be a path through a forest, or the way to a village). Using these ingredients, draft a short story beginning:

'Once upon a time ...'

026

Opening lines

'Once upon a time' is perhaps the most recognisable way of beginning a fairy tale. Hans Christian Andersen, however, used many variations in order to set his stories in motion. Consider the following:

'Far away, towards the east, in India...'
(**The Philosopher's Stone**, 1859)

'You must attend to the commencement of this story...'
(**The Snow Queen**, 1845)

'There was once an Emperor...'
(**The Beetle Who Went on His Travels**, 1861)

Exercise: Devise opening lines, as alternatives to 'once upon a time', that would be suitable for the beginnings of fairy tales. Try to think of five.

#027

The cold of winter

Hans Christian Andersen's *The Snow Queen* is full of the chills of winter. He uses phrases such as 'shining and glittering ice' and offers unusual imagery, such as snowflakes 'like great white chickens'.

Exercise: Try to create a cold, wintry effect in a single, long paragraph of descriptive writing. Select a setting (for example, a hillside, street, garden, suburban street or wood) and include as many words as possible that indicate the season, such as 'chill', 'bitter', 'freezing', 'ice-cold' and 'numbing'. Also make use of colours, such as grey, dun and white. Keep the writing tight. It could form the basis for a story.

LEWIS CARROLL

BORN: 27 January, 1832
DIED: 14 January, 1898
WRITING: Fantasy adventure; nonsense poetry
KEY WORK: *Alice's Adventures in Wonderland*

Reverend Charles Lutwidge Dodgson, otherwise known as Lewis Carroll, was a writer, mathematician, Anglican deacon and photographer. His hugely popular books have secured his reputation as a master of the literary nonsense genre.

The precocious boy

Born into the large family of a Church of England country parson, Lewis Carroll was a home-educated child, and, as befitted a time when self-entertainment was paramount, he wrote poems and stories from an early age. His intellectual ability quickly shone through and he went on to study, and later teach, mathematics at Christ Church College, Oxford University. He published books about mathematics during this time. Despite being plagued by a lifelong stammer, he led a busy social life, which included associations with such Pre-Raphaelites as Rossetti, Holman Hunt and Millais.

His pseudonym, Lewis Carroll, first appeared in a publication in 1856. When a new dean arrived at the College with his family – the Liddells – Carroll began to spend time with them. In the children's company, he went on many outings into the local countryside, during which he invented stories for them, including one about the daughter, Alice Liddell.

The Alice books

Alice Liddell begged him to write down the tale, and after a lengthy delay he presented her with a handwritten, illustrated version of the story. Albeit with a different title, it signalled the moment when *Alice's Adventures in Wonderland* was born. The book, complete with Sir John Tenniel's illustrations, was published in 1865. It gradually gained popularity worldwide and changed Carroll's college-cloistered life forever.

Alice's Adventures in Wonderland, commonly known as *Alice in Wonderland*, recounts a girl's adventures after she follows a formally attired white rabbit down a rabbit hole. 'Oh dear! Oh dear! I shall be too late!' is the rabbit's famous utterance. So Alice

Carroll had to contend with a stammer his entire life. In his books, Carroll visualised stammer-free imaginary worlds, while in reality it interfered with his clerical duties and social life. Interestingly, the stammer is said to have vanished when Carroll was in conversation with children.

A detail of an illustration by Charles Robinson from *Alice's Adventures in Wonderland* (1907).

enters a fantasy world of weird people, strange happenings and fantastic anthropomorphic creatures.

Alice in Wonderland is a timeless story, and an enduring tale. Carroll, wearing his logician's hat, takes the story far into the literary nonsense genre. The first print run was destroyed at Carroll's request, because he was dissatisfied with the production quality. Initially, the book's reviews were poor, with more credit given to Tenniel's illustrations than to the author. By the end of the 19th century, its place as a classic was assured. It has been reissued repeatedly, and illustrated by such artists as Salvador Dali, Arthur Rackham, Peter Blake and Max Ernst. Countless versions have appeared as films, and on stage and TV.

Famous characters and set pieces

The book teems with characters, such as the Dodo, the Duck, The Hatter, Bill the Lizard and many more, all based on people Carroll knew. Buildings in Oxford were the basis for places visited by Alice as she travels through Wonderland. There are scenes in the story that have famously entered the collective consciousness, such

'A book of that extremely rare kind which will belong to all the generations to come until language becomes obsolete.'

– Sir Walter Beasant on *Alice's Adventures in Wonderland*

as the Hatter's Tea-Party, in which Alice takes part in logic games, word play, riddles and nonsense. The book contains poems, parodies ('Twinkle, Twinkle, Little Bat'), concrete poetry (the mouse's tale told in the shape of a mouse's tail), songs, puns, jokes, jests, magic and of course nonsense. There is a great deal of eating and drinking, and the book fizzes with energy. It is a cornucopia of ideas, and above all it is great fun for everyone – children and adults.

Today, the writing appears lengthy and garrulous, yet the magic remains. An industry of interpretation and comment has grown up around the Alice books, not least about Lewis Carroll himself.

028

Nonsense verse

Like Roald Dahl and A. A. Milne, Lewis Carroll often broke into verse in his stories. In *Through the Looking-Glass*, Alice discovers a book with a poem that looks unreadable. She has to hold it before a looking-glass before she can read it properly. The poem in question is the now famous 'Jabberwocky', in which Carroll created a fearsome creature, the Jabberwock. In the poem, he invents many words, including 'slithy toves', 'vorpal', 'uffish', 'galumphing', 'frabjous', 'brillig' – all of them utter nonsense, yet brilliant.

Exercise: Release your powers of creativity and make up ten new words that will appeal to young readers. Now compose a four-line verse with the rhyme scheme A, B, A, B. Use as many of the newly minted words as possible. It isn't easy, but is worth persevering with. The result may be surprising!

029

A strange meeting

Alice met many strange people and creatures in Wonderland, not least the Queen of Hearts and the Mock Turtle. She had conversations with all of them.

Exercise: Imagine she is about to encounter a new creature in Wonderland. Decide what it is: A dog? An elephant? An ant? An owl? A shark?

Write a conversation between this new creature and Alice. Begin with a sentence or two, explaining Alice's initial surprise at the encounter. Give the conversation a touch of Lewis Carroll's mock-formality, including word play, puns and a dash of strangeness. End the conversation formally, before Alice moves on.

030

That shrinking feeling

In *Alice's Adventures in Wonderland*, Alice sees a little bottle with 'Drink Me' printed on a paper label. She does just that, and shrinks until she is 'only ten inches high'. It means she is now able to go 'through the little door into that lovely garden'.

Exercise: Draft the outline for a short story about a large creature that, after eating crusts of stale bread, shrinks to a fraction of its size, enabling it to go places it couldn't go before and confront new challenges and dangers. Now write the story in 250 words.

031

All on a summer's day

At the beginning of *Alice's Adventures in Wonderland*, we see Alice sitting beside her sister on the bank, tired of having nothing to do, when the White Rabbit runs by.

Exercise: What would have happened if the White Rabbit *hadn't* appeared and there had been no adventures in Wonderland? How would Alice have amused herself that hot summer's day? Compose a short passage, describing how Alice wanders away from the bank and what she does.

ASTRID LINDGREN

BORN: 14 November, 1907
DIED: 28 January, 2002
WRITING: Fantasy adventure
KEY WORK: *Pippi Longstocking*

Astrid Lindgren was a Swedish author, who, despite early rejection, became a hugely successful children's author thanks to her book series featuring such characters as Pippi Longstocking, Karlsson-on-the-Roof and the six Bullerby children.

A single mother

Like J. K. Rowling, Astrid Lindgren was a single mother who was experiencing difficult times and financial hardship when she began writing for children. She earned a living as a journalist and then as a secretary, before marrying her employer. In order to amuse her sick, bed-ridden young daughter, Astrid Lindgren made up stories about a feisty, adventurous girl, Pippi Longstocking.

The character eventually featured in a book-length tale that was initially rejected, before being published in 1945. It was the forerunner to a number of book series that have remained international bestsellers. They have spawned a number of films and been adapted for TV.

Pippi Longstocking

Her characters are the cornerstone of Lindgren's writing. Pippi Longstocking, one of her most famous creations, is a girl with

whom young readers immediately identified. Such was the character's attractiveness that the readers hungered for more. Three books in the series were published between 1945 and 1948. A further six followed in the years 1969–1975, and the final two appeared in 1979 and 2000.

Pippi Longstocking was a girl before her time. She is, rather startlingly for 1945, a thoroughly adventurous, strong-minded, boisterously upbeat, independent girl who possesses super-human strength and lives on her own with only a monkey (Mr. Nilsson) and a horse for company. She gets into all manner of adventurous and crazily hilarious scrapes. Pippi is also remarkable for her appearance: carrot red hair, long sticky-out pigtails, and those signature long colourful (and odd) socks: 'On her long thin legs she wore long stockings, one brown and the other black'.

Years before Pippi Longstocking emerged, Astrid Lindgren compiled 17 volumes of war diaries beginning in September 1939 and ending with the cessation of World War II in 1945. The handwritten diaries are peppered with press cuttings and family photographs.

A still from the Swedish television series *Pippi Långstrump*, based on Lindgren's books.

The girl's prized possessions (the animals apart) are a suitcase filled with gold coins, and a large chest of drawers containing various small treasures. Other characters include her friends next door, Tommy and Anika.

Pippi Longstocking, like Peter Pan, does not want to grow up. She displays an irreverent attitude towards adult authority: this is a distinguishing trait in many of Astrid Lindgren's characters.

The writing style

Astrid Lindgren is the narrator, and reports what happens in the third person. The stories are related in simple, straightforward, plainly written sentences. The authorial voice is crystal clear. Information about Pippi's background, for example, is disclosed gradually, in a natural and unforced manner, as the tale unfolds. The pace of the narrative is speedy, yet the author has the knack of seeming unrushed and unhurried – not an easy trick to pull off.

Each chapter (there are 11 in the first Pippi Longstocking book) is a separate adventure. Chapter 7, for example, begins, 'A circus had come to the little town', and so introduces yet another of Pippi's extraordinary and energetic adventures.

Dialogue is plentiful, and in each instance it is short and succinct. Between the dialogue, the narrator's assured writing explains simply what's happening: 'Some of the people helped to untie the knot and free the boy. Pippi really could tie knots! She learned that at sea.' That is a good example of explanatory writing, with an additional piece of background information given in the last sentence.

> *'Her niche in children's fantasy remains both secure and exalted. Her stories and images can never be forgotten.'*
> — *The Encyclopaedia of Fantasy*

What a girl!

Pippi Longstocking is unforgettable, not only for her adventures but also for her appearance: the hair colour, those sticky-out pigtails, the odd long socks and her nose 'the shape of a very small potato'.

Exercise: Write a description of a ten-year-old girl who doesn't look anything like Pippi Longstocking, yet has that girl's personality: strong-willed, assertive, fearless, super-confident and independent. In the description, concentrate on her looks and clothes, as well as her mannerisms. She needs to be a character that readers won't easily forget.

033

Negotiation

The two children who live next door to Pippi Longstocking, Tommy and Annika, are well behaved and come from a conformist and conventional family. What must their mother think about them having exciting adventures with wild, unpredictable Pippi?

Exercise: Compose a conversation between two children and their mother. The children are desperate to play with a girl or boy their mother thinks is a bad influence. The mother is a smooth and determined talker. The children struggle to convince her. Through dialogue, show how the debate is resolved. Write in the third person.

#034

An ideas circle

In *Pippi Longstocking*, the feisty girl is counting her gold pieces when two tramps turn up at her house. Seeing the money, the greedy men plan to rob the girl. Pippi must outsmart them, which of course she does!

Exercise: Think of ways (simple or ingenious) by which a girl could outwit and get rid of thieves who have entered her house. Write your ideas around the circle. Then think of two other situations when a girl has to rely on her wit and imagination to get out of a difficult situation, and complete the same task for those.

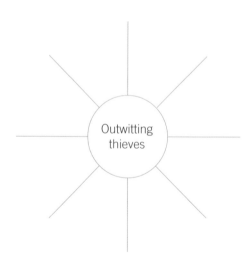

Outwitting
thieves

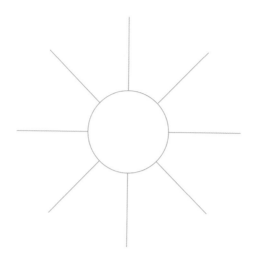

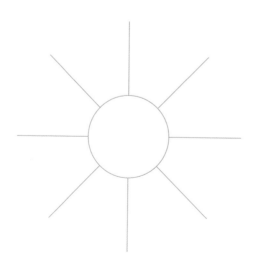

#035

Open the suitcase

Pippi's suitcase is one of her prized possessions. It is filled with gold coins. In children's stories, there is often a box or a chest that, once discovered and opened, reveals exciting things. Jim Hawkins, in Robert Louis Stevenson's epic adventure *Treasure Island*, finds an old map when he opens Captain Billy Bones' seaman's chest. It proves to be a central item, an emblem, in the story.

Exercise: Take the following premise: Two cousins explore an attic at Grandma's house, where they find a dusty old wooden box. When opened, it reveals surprises. Write an account of the two children's exploration of the attic, their conversation, the discovery of the wooden box, and what they find inside. Concentrate on creating a rather shivery, spooky atmosphere. Make use of sounds, such as squeaks, creaks, rustlings and whooshing noises.

E. B. WHITE

BORN: 11 July, 1899
DIED: 1 October, 1985
WRITING: Fantasy realism
KEY WORK: *Charlotte's Web*

Prior to writing stories for children, Elwyn Brooks White was a journalist, poet and editor of an English-language style guide. Three of his children's books, most notably Charlotte's Web, *proved massively popular and were translated worldwide.*

Shy and professional

A former soldier, and graduate from Cornell University, E. B. White moved into journalism. He became a reporter, columnist and sketch writer who was employed on the staff of the literary magazine *The New Yorker*. He was a shy person, disinclined to seek publicity. James Thurber, in his book *Credos and Curios*, described him as a quiet man 'who would slip out of the office (at *The New Yorker*) via the fire-escape to avoid visitors whom he didn't know'.

In 1959 he edited *The Elements of Style*, a guide to usage of the English language. In 1978 he won the Pulitzer Prize 'for his letters, essays and the full body of his work'.

In the late 1930s, White tried his hand at children's fiction. His first book, *Stuart Little* (1945), received a lukewarm welcome.

Charlotte's Web (1952) proved more popular, and the two books eventually received high acclaim. A third book, *The Trumpet of the Swan* (1973), was another award winner. He won the Laura Ingalls Wilder Medal in 1979 for a 'substantial and lasting contribution to children's literature'.

Stuart Little *and* Charlotte's Web

Like Lewis Carroll, E. B. White's writing for young readers began when children – in this instance, his many nieces and nephews – asked him to tell them a story. White wrote down a tale from an idea he had about 'a tiny boy who acted rather like a mouse', born to human parents. *Stuart Little* was thus created, with its realistic fantasy about a talking mouse. As with Maurice Sendak, the editor Ursula Nordstrom proved an important figure. She enjoyed White's next offering, *Charlotte's Web*, and the book was published in 1952, three years after White began writing it.

White's literary duties kept him in New York City, but he relished his other home, a farmhouse in rural North Brooklin, Maine, USA, where he could indulge his love of wildlife. It is said that seeing a spider spin an egg sac in the farmhouse barn was the inspiration for *Charlotte's Web*.

White photographed in 1977 at his home in Brooklin, Maine.

> *'As a piece of work it is just about perfect, and just magical in the way it is done.'*
>
> – **Eudora Welty reviewing *Charlotte's Web* in *The New York Times*.**

The story revolves around farmyard creatures: a runt of a pig, Wilbur, and his friendship with an intelligent barn spider, Charlotte, who spins messages of encouragement in her webs. A rat, Templeton, offers comic relief, as do some of the humans. A girl, Fern Arable, is the only human in the book who fully understands the creatures' conversations.

From the beginning there is tension regarding the piglet's future: will he be killed? The story relates the efforts, not least Charlotte's, to save him. In the end it is Charlotte who dies ('no one was with her when she died'), a truly emotional, tear-jerking moment. Wilbur the piglet survives.

Garth Williams' original black and white drawings beautifully illuminate the text.

The stylist

White, in his introduction to *The Elements of Style*, says good writing should have 'cleanliness, accuracy, and brevity'. These attributes, honed from many years as a professional writer with periodicals, is clearly demonstrated in his children's books. The text is very readable, being simply stated yet detailed. He was a careful, deliberate craftsman who took considerable time to produce his books. He was a master of description and used repetition skilfully, and he enjoyed the use of antithesis – the inclusion of opposing words in the same sentence. About New York City he once wrote, 'It even managed to reach the highest point in the sky at the lowest moment of the depression'. He was a witty writer who said, 'Writing is an act of faith, not a trick of grammar'.

#036

A master of description

In *Charlotte's Web*, E. B. White's descriptions are filled with glorious detail: 'In early summer there are plenty of things for a child to eat and drink and suck and chew. Dandelion stems are full of milk, clover heads are loaded with nectar, the Frigidaire is full of ice-cold drinks.' The writing is good enough to taste.

Exercise: Think back to a time as a child when you had some really wonderful things to eat and drink. It may have been at a birthday party, at Christmas, on an outing or at a picnic. Make a list of all the things you can remember about the food and drink. Using this list, compose a paragraph that mirrors E. B. White's description. Make it factual, yet rich in detail.

#037

Sending messages

Charlotte, the barn spider, was highly skilled at spinning messages into her webs as a means of communicating.

Exercise: See if you can devise ways in which other creature characters in a story could come up with original ways of communicating. For instance, a cat scratching messages with its claws on the kitchen table, or a cockroach leaving messages by scuttling through the dust on the attic floor.

Try to invents methods of communication for:

- A brown rat
- A lost elephant
- A guard dog
- A seagull
- A hedgehog
- A snake

038

A death

'No one was with her when she died.' It's the last line of chapter 21 in *Charlotte's Web* and provides a sad, poignant and heart-rending moment. In the build-up to that sorrowful line, E. B. White handles the narrative superbly. There is no dialogue or authorial comment, just a simple description of the scene. It is emotion under the author's control.

Exercise: Write a passage, suitable for children, about a creature's death you have witnessed or experienced. It could feature a pet or an insect (like Charlotte), perhaps in a road accident, or inspired by something you have read about (for example, the death of a panda in a zoo).

You are the narrator. Like E. B. White, keep yourself out of the story. Just report the tragic event.

LAURA INGALLS WILDER

BORN: 7 February, 1867
DIED: 10 February, 1957
WRITING: Social realism/adventure
KEY WORK: *The Little House on the Prairie*

Laura Ingalls Wilder is an American writer well known for her books based on her life as the child of a settler family on the American frontier in the 19th century. They have remained very popular, spawning a long-running TV series.

A settler family childhood

In 1869, when Laura Ingalls Wilder was an infant, the Wilder family set out from their home in Wisconsin as pioneers looking to settle in the Osage Indian reservation, on what was then regarded as the American frontier. They had no legal rights and soon returned to Big Woods, Wisconsin. Thereafter, further house moves occurred before the family settled in a homestead on the plains of Dakota. Wilder became a teacher at 16, married at 18 and lived a life of financial uncertainty. Not until 1911, at the age of 44, did she become a newspaper columnist and take up writing.

Her daughter, Rose Lane, herself a published novelist, encouraged her mother to write about her childhood experiences, as a source of income after the family finances were devastated in the stock market crash of 1929. Wilder wrote *Pioneer Girl*, which was rejected, but she took on board the publisher's advice to greatly expand the story and make it accessible for children.

In 1932, when Wilder was in her 60s, *Little House in the Big Woods* was published, and further instalments quickly followed, notably *The Little House on the Prairie* in 1935. The series became very popular. On five occasions the books were runners-up for the Newbery Medal. In recognition of her work, The Laura Ingalls Wilder Medal was instituted for authors or illustrators whose books, published in the USA, have made

---

– **Nancy Koupal, a publishing director involved with the publication of *Pioneer Girl*, has pointed to Wilder's**

'Gift for descriptive prose and a true love of the prairie landscape'.

Before turning to fiction and beginning work on her *Little House* books, Wilder honed a plainly stated literary style by contributing a biweekly column to the *Missouri Ruralist* between 1911 and 1924, in which she wrote observations of and stated sensible opinions about farming, marriage and country life.

The farmhouse on Rocky Ridge Farm, where Wilder wrote the *Little House* books.

'A substantial and lasting contribution to literature for children'. Recipients included E. B. White (1970), Dr. Seuss (1980) and Maurice Sendak (1983).

Heading west

The Little House on the Prairie, the third volume in the series, recounts the family heading west in search of wide open spaces: 'They were going to Indian country, because, as Pa said, "There were too many people in Big Woods now"'. The author is the narrator, even though Laura is a child character in the story. In 26 chapters we learn about the day-to-day life of the extended family of settlers, their trials and tribulations, adventures, difficulties and the dangers faced. The story is part diary, part nature observation and part social history. The descriptiveness is particularly vivid: 'Once a shadow floated across the grass, and every gopher vanished. A hawk was sailing overhead. It was so close that Laura saw its cruel round eye turned downwards to look at her.' Wilder's writing is economic and cleanly expressed: you feel as if you are there. It is a book that can be enjoyed by children and adults alike.

A steady flow

The writing has a steady yet relentless flow about it. It is easy to read, while at the same time it is dense with detail, events, observations and dialogue. The characters are solidly drawn. The rolling, unfolding story envelopes the reader; it is like a warm, comfortable and comforting blanket wrapping itself around you.

Wilder's style was based on simple sentences. She built detail patiently and visually, and her home-spun style reflects the entries from her own diaries written as a pioneer girl. After her death the popularity of the books continued to grow. They have been continuously in print and widely translated. Many of her earlier writings were collected, edited and published posthumously.

Some critics have accused the *Prairie* series of sentimentality and of romanticising the life of settlers, all the more so when Wilder's original *Pioneer Girl* was published, with its diary entries recording the warts-and-all harshness of frontier life in the nineteenth century.

039

Dear diary

Laura Ingalls Wilder's diary entries when she was growing up in her settler family became, in effect, her writing apprenticeship. She was able to use them as a resource and a reminder of her day-to-day experiences on the prairie.

Exercise: Invent a week's diary entries for a family journeying into open spaces – a mountainous region, plain or desert. As Wilder did, concentrate on observations of the surrounding nature. Write in the third person 'we', as if you are a member of the family reporting what happens.

040

Weather

Weather, and the changing of the seasons, was of great interest to Laura Ingalls Wilder. *The Little House on the Prairie* is filled with her observations: 'Cold rains were falling. Day after day the rain fell, pattering on the roof and pouring from the eaves.' And, 'Winter ended at last. There was a softer note in the sound of the wind, and the bitter cold had gone.'

Exercise: Write a weather report for the four seasons, a brief paragraph for each one. Try to emulate Laura Ingalls Wilder's use of simple language, at the same time making accurate, clear observations. If anything, her writing is downplayed rather than excitable. Can you achieve that homespun quality?

#041

A scream in the night

'A Scream in the Night', chapter 20 in *The Little House on the Prairie*, describes how a mysterious, frightening noise wakes the children.

Exercise: Imagine you are a child in bed on a stormy night. Suddenly you are awoken by a terrifying scream. Write an internal monologue in the first person. What was it you heard? What questions fly through your head? What about the darkness? What is the weather doing? The monologue should flow breathlessly and build up tension, until the matter is resolved, or not.

#042

Constructing a shelter

In *The Little House on the Prairie* we see exactly how Pa builds a log house. Shelter from the elements or from danger features in many stories for children: castaway Robinson Crusoe constructed a hut on the island and the Hobbit has his hole in the ground.

Exercise: In a story you are writing for children, the characters need to construct a shelter. The story could be set in a forest, or at the edge of a lake, or beside the sea. Choose a location and then write ten-step instructions on how they should set about the task.

Location:

1

2

3

4

5

6

7

8

9

10

C. S. LEWIS

BORN: 29 November, 1898
DIED: 22 November, 1963
WRITING: Fantasy adventure
KEY WORK: *The Chronicles of Narnia* series

Clive Staples Lewis was a major intellectual figure in the twentieth century. His series of fantasy novels for children, The Chronicles of Narnia, *was translated around the world, and gained further popularity on stage, screen, television and radio.*

Sagas and myths

As a boy growing up in Belfast, Northern Ireland, C. S. Lewis was fascinated by anthropomorphic animals, such as Beatrix Potter's talking rabbits. As a teenager he immersed himself in the Icelandic sagas and Norse and Greek mythology. A brilliant academic pupil, he studied at Oxford University before accepting the chair of Mediaeval and Renaissance Literature at Cambridge University, where he remained throughout his career. He was a close friend of the high-fantasy writer J. R. R. Tolkien.

He wrote many books for adults, including science fiction (*The Space Trilogy*) but is best remembered for his seven-book series of fantasy stories for children, *The Chronicles of Narnia*, with their mix of magic, mythical beasts, talking animals and human characters. The series has profoundly influenced children's fantasy literature ever since.

Lewis won the Carnegie Medal in 1956 for, appropriately, the final book in the series, *The Last Battle*.

A fictional world

Written between 1949 and 1954, the seven books known collectively as *The Chronicles of Narnia* are now regarded as modern classics. At the rate of a book per year, C. S. Lewis created a complete fictional world, Narnia. Woven into the books are Christian themes, characters from Greek and Roman mythology and traditional British and Irish folk tales. The stories tell how various children play roles in the fortunes of Narnia.

The seven books span the entire history of Narnia, from its creation (*The Magician's Nephew*) to its eventual destruction (*The Last Battle*). The books were not published in chronological order: *The Magician's Nephew*, the fourth book the series, was in effect a prequel.

By June 1961, C. S. Lewis' health was declining, and he was forced to retire from his post at Cambridge University. He died on 22 November, 1963, but the event went largely unnoticed by the media due to the assassination in Dallas of the U.S. president, John F. Kennedy, less than an hour later.

A view of Magdalene College, Cambridge, where Lewis worked from 1954 until the end of his career.

Human characters flit in and out of the stories, appearing in different books. The only character who features in all seven books is Aslan, a talking lion.

The first book
The Lion, the Witch and the Wardrobe launched the series. It has a terrific beginning: four members of a family (the Pevensie children), who are evacuees from London during World War II, are sent to the safety of an old mansion in the countryside. Upon exploring the house, they discover a wardrobe through which they enter the magical world of Narnia, which is held in the grip of perpetual winter – with no Christmas! The story revolves around their adventures assisting Aslan the Lion to save Narnia from the evil clutches of the White Witch.

'You are never too old to set another goal or to dream a new dream.'

– C. S. Lewis

As with Roald Dahl, C. S. Lewis was inventive with names. In the various books we meet Polly Plummer, Digory Kirke, Jill Pole, Eustace Scrubb, Trumpkin the Dwarf, Puddleglum and Mr. Tumnus, among a vast gallery of characters.

Richly detailed and imaginative
Lewis wrote at what seems like top speed. This is reflected in the breathless pace of the telling. It certainly keeps readers on their toes, eager to find out what happens next. He narrates in the third person and intersperses snippets of dialogue between long paragraphs, which are rich with detail. The author's imaginative powers are constantly in gear.

A short passage from *The Lion, the Witch and the Wardrobe* demonstrates how Lewis unhesitatingly, almost restlessly, pushed the story forwards: 'While he was still chewing away, the first dwarf came back and announced that the sledge was ready. The White Witch rose and went out, ordering Edmund to go with her. The snow was again falling as they came into the courtyard.'

043

Questions and answers

In *The Lion, the Witch and the Wardrobe*, the children are keen to glean information from an old professor about the mysterious wardrobe that leads to the magical world of Narnia.

Exercise: Two children have the task of gathering information about a seaside amusement park. It is in preparation for a feature they are writing for their school newspaper. They interview the park owner in the head teacher's room. In the left columns, write the questions the children ask, and in the left columns, the park owner's replies.

Question	Answer

Question	Answer

044

A build-up description

Lucy, the youngest of the four Pevensie children, is entranced by a winter scene in Narnia: '[...] the dazzling brightness of the frozen river with its waterfalls of ice and at the white masses of the tree-tops and the great glaring moon and the countless stars.'

Exercise: Choose a season (it doesn't have to be winter) and compose a build-up description of a scene (day or night). Make the writing run on and on without punctuation, each observation joined to the next by 'and', as C. S. Lewis did in the above example. Make the list as long as possible. The result can be powerfully effective.

045

A portal to another world

The idea of a portal into another, imaginary world is a familiar narrative device. C. S. Lewis sends the Pevensie children into another world through a magical wardrobe.

Exercise: Two characters (for example, a girl and her boy cousin) are on a family visit to an old castle. They wander away from the group and discover a rusty iron ring set in a flagstone. When turned in a certain way, the flagstone grates open and the children see a flight of stone steps descending into the gloom. In trepidation they go down the steps.

Write a 350-word story about the strange world the two children discover. Make use of the senses: sound, smell, touch and sight. Who, or what, do they encounter? What happens? At the end, the children climb back up the stone steps.

046

The wrecked mansion

In *The Lion, the Witch and the Wardrobe* the four children tramp through the snow and arrive at Mr. Tumnus's cave home in Narnia, only to find it wrecked. The door has been smashed in and everything in his cosy home is broken or destroyed.

Exercise: Use the following scenario as the basis for a ghost story: three children push open the heavy oak door of an abandoned mansion to discover it in a state of dereliction. They enter with trepidation.

Begin the ghost story (350 words) by describing what they see (for example, spiders and other creatures, spooky portraits, a headless suit of armour, frayed carpets). What apparitions do they encounter? How does the story end?

EOIN COLFER

BORN: 14 May, 1965
DIED: N/A
WRITING: Fantasy
KEY WORK: *Artemis Fowl* series

Eoin Colfer is an Irish author whose Artemis Fowl *series of fantasy adventure novels for older children has regularly featured in* The New York Times *bestsellers lists.*

Redefining the fairytale

Colfer was a school teacher when he created the character Artemis Fowl, a 12-year-old child prodigy who is the son of an Irish crime lord and a criminal mastermind in his own right. The immediate success of the first book, *Artemis Fowl* (2001), led him to take up writing full-time. The series currently stands at eight books. The most recent, *Artemis Fowl: The Last Guardian*, was published in 2012.

At the start of the first book, Artemis sets out to kidnap a fairy, Captain Holly Short of the LEPrecon Unit, for a gold ransom. The author has described the narrative as 'Die Hard with fairies', referring to the 1988 film, and as such has set about redefining the traditional fairy story.

Artemis and his minder, Butler, are ultra-contemporary characters. For them, criss-crossing the planet is a common experience, they are competent with weaponry and are IT-savvy. The narrative is alive with mentions of PCs, flatbed scanners, Powerbook screens and surfing the Internet. Yet the books are not geeky or nerdish. They are taut, event-filled stories with strongly drawn characters – very much books of the present day.

The characters

The books' characters are particularly well defined. Colfer is excellent at physical descriptions, which he uses to clearly define his characters' roles in the novels. For example, Artemis is 'white as a vampire'. Why? Because of long hours spent in front of the monitor. He has dedicated his life to criminal activities and is set to lead the Fowl crime empire, which has been established for generations. If *Harry Potter* stands at the noble end of young-adult fiction, *Artemis Fowl* occupies the dastardly end.

Colfer worked abroad for four years in Saudi Arabia, Tunisia and Italy, and drew upon these experiences in writing his first book, *Benny and Omar* (1998). In it he recounts the growing friendship between Benny, who takes for granted Western comforts, and Omar, a local orphan who struggles to attain life's basics.

Eoin Colfer continues to write bestselling children's books, including three titles in his new WARP series.

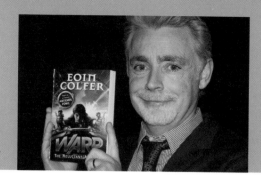

'*Hugely enjoyable, just the right mix of fantasy, humor, gadgets and thrills*'

— *The Fantasy Book Review*

Butler, the minder who comes from a long line of Butlers devoted to the Fowl criminal dynasty, has 'Two shrike throwing knives in his boots [...] garrotte wire in his watch and three stun grenades concealed in various pockets'. Captain Holly Short, the fairy, has a nose 'that was long and hooked under two slitted golden eyes'. Colfer's character descriptions are incredibly vivid and are magnetic to readers because of their visual strength: '[Short's] ears were pointed, and the alcohol addiction had melted her skin like putty'. She has 'long tapered fingers perfect for wrapping around a buzz baton'. Some fairy!

Other characters, such as Julius Root, Foaly, Mulch Diggums, Grub Kelp, the trolls, and the tunnel dwarves, slip in and out of the action, and they too are sharply portrayed.

Plot and language

The third-person narration switches between chapters, at one time following the human characters' exploits and at another the actions of the fairy. The underlying themes are greed and conflict, and there's no shortage of either.

Eoin Colfer creates sinewy and twisting plots: locations change, action moves swiftly, and characters arrive and depart at speed. The author, like a skilled puppeteer, maintains all of this without getting into a knot. His use of language is direct, terse and brief, which contributes to the ferocious pace of the narrative. The characters' exchanges, often involving the use of technology, are dramatic. The writing fizzes and crackles with their exchanges. Throughout the narrative there is an edge of humor, an underlying, knowing smirk.

Dastardly acts

'Artemis cracked his knuckles. Time to do what he did best – plot dastardly acts.' So ends chapter 2 in *Artemis Fowl*. It is a cliff-hanger, enticing the reader to find out about Artemis's 'dastardly acts' in chapter 3.

Exercise: Create a new character (a boy or girl, or perhaps a talking animal) who is evil-minded. He or she will need an original name. Writing quickly, list five dastardly acts they might undertake. It could be a supermarket robbery or loosening the wheel nuts on someone's bicycle. Choose one of these acts and write a chapter (300 words) about the act, incorporating quick-fire dialogue and the use of modern technology.

#048   *Battle*

In *Artemis Fowl* the human character, Butler, straps on a medieval suit of armour and goes toe to toe with the troll, with medieval and modern weaponry at his disposal. The troll has ten extending talons and venom-tipped tusks. A battle royale ensues.

Exercise: Describe in vivid terms, and with no holds barred, a fight between a zombie and a human zombie hunter, deciding first which age group you are writing for. Both parties have weaponry, either on or within themselves. Include detailed descriptions of the injuries (there will be gore), but ensure that the content is age appropriate.

049

Two-way take

Eoin Colfer repeatedly switches viewpoint over the course of a story. In one chapter we read about what Artemis Fowl is doing, and in the next we get Holly Short's version of events. Each perspective provides a different take on what is happening in the story. It is a narrative device that has been used before, for example, by John Fowles in his bestselling novel *The Butterfly Collector*.

Exercise: Write a fantasy story (two paragraphs) about a boy criminal who kidnaps a girl and imprisons her in a castle dungeon. Both paragraphs should be written in the first person, the first from the boy's viewpoint, the second from the girl's viewpoint.

J. R. R. TOLKIEN

BORN: 3 January, 1892
DIED: 2 September, 1973
WRITING: High-fantasy
KEY WORK: *The Lord of the Rings*

Born in South Africa, John Ronald Reuel Tolkien was an English university professor, poet, philologist and author of the classics The Hobbit, The Lord of the Rings *and* The Silmarillion. *He has been called 'the father of modern high-fantasy literature'.*

Steeped in language

From an early age, Tolkien was a voracious reader and developed a life-long love of language. A brilliant scholar at Oxford University, his academic life was interrupted when he served as a soldier in the British Army in the First World War. Notably, he fought at the Battle of the Somme in 1916, before being wounded and invalided home.

All the while he continued writing and studying, and in 1925 was appointed Professor of Anglo-Saxon at Oxford, where he stayed until his retirement in 1959. While at Oxford he was a member of a group called The Inklings, which included the author C. S. Lewis, with whom he formed a close friendship. At University Tolkien was a charismatic figure. The poet W. H. Auden, wrote, 'What an unforgettable experience it was for me as an undergraduate, hearing you recite Beowulf. The voice was the voice of Gandalf.'

Tolkien steeped himself in literature and gathered a vast knowledge of Germanic tales, Old English literature, poetry and mythology. He continued writing, and his academic career and his literary work became inseparable.

The books for children

In the 1930s Tolkien started work on a tale for children. It began when, in the middle of his academic work, he took an empty sheet of paper and wrote, 'In a hole in the ground there lived a Hobbit'. That is the now famous opening for *The Hobbit*, which was published in 1937. It received widespread critical acclaim and was nominated for the Carnegie Medal. It attracted adult readers as well as children, and the publisher urged Tolkien to produce a sequel. It was a long time coming, but eventually the *The Lord of the Rings* saw the light of day. It addressed an older audience than *The Hobbit*.

As a schoolboy, Tolkien's outstanding linguistic gifts enabled him to learn Latin, Greek and other ancient and modern languages, including Gothic and Finnish. Purely for fun he made up his own languages, a talent that featured in his high-fantasy writings.

In June 2015, a first edition of *The Hobbit* sold at auction in London for more than $200,000.

The Lord of the Rings is considered to be a single novel across three books (rather than a trilogy of separate novels). The first book, *The Fellowship of the Ring*, was published in July 1954; the second, *The Two Towers* in November the same year; and the final part, *The Return of the King* in October 1955. Together, they represent a colossal achievement, not only due to their epic length and unforgettable characters – from Bilbo Baggins to Gollum and the wizard Gandalf – but also for their scholarship, invention, complexity and above all for Tolkien's soaring imagination. Where *The Hobbit* was very much a story for children, *The Lord of the Rings* trilogy appealed to a wider audience. The books have been adapted as hugely successful films.

'Many children make up, or begin to make up, imaginary languages. I have been at it since I could write.'

– J. R. R. Tolkien

A style apart

Tolkien's books have assumed a cult status. Around them, an industry of examination and interpretation has flourished. Yet, despite the remarkable amount of detail Tolkien provides on the myriad characters and the complex events of the novel, his prose remains clear and controlled. For example, Tolkien writes, 'The Company spent that night in the great cavernous hall, huddled close together in a corner to escape the draught: there seemed to be a steady inflow of chill air through the eastern archway'.

The clarity notwithstanding, Tolkien's writing is also minutely detailed and his descriptions at times lavish. This runs contrary, perhaps, to a contemporary preference for stories that move at top speed, leading some to consider such lavishness as ponderous, even overblown.

050

First lines

As we've seen, the first line of *The Hobbit* is memorable: 'In a hole in the ground there lived a Hobbit'. It is a great 'hook', encouraging the young reader to ask, 'What is a Hobbit?' and 'Why does it live in a hole?' Other writers featured in *Children's Writer's Notebook* do something similar. For example, E. B. White's *Charlotte's Web* (see pages 96–97) opens, '"Where's Papa going with that axe?" said Fern'.

Exercise: Using the following prompts, create some opening lines that command the reader's attention:
- A dragon in its cavern
- An astronaut drifting towards a black hole in space
- A dog in a town park – at midnight
- A girl and her horse lost in a blizzard
- Little Red Riding Hood entering the deep, dark wood
- A mermaid discovering a pirate's sunken ship
- A cow jumping over the moon

#051 *Naming names*

Tolkien loved naming places, things and characters. His books are crammed with such imaginative names as Frodo, the Orcs of Mordor, Middle-earth, the Misty Mountains, Gorbag, the Shire, Bag End – the list is endless.

Exercise: Draw up a list of startlingly good names, which would work well in children's stories, for the following:

- A one-eared teddy bear in a child's bedroom
- A pirate captain (you could use the following formula: a first name, two middle names, and then your own surname spelled backwards)
- The newly discovered range of mountains on Mars
- A farmyard cat and her four kittens
- A mythical beast that roams the Arabian desert
- Three friends (first and last names) who go to explore a ruined mansion
- A thief and his accomplice who rob people on trains in London

#052

Creating a landscape

Tolkien's imagination was boundless when it came to creating vistas and landscapes. His descriptions are rich with mountains, cliffs, defiles, inland seas, plains, passes, caverns, rivers, waterfalls, wastes, marshes and forests, many of which he gives names to. In addition to these are buildings, forts, watchtowers, ramparts, castles and halls.

Exercise: Using the blank space below, sketch a map of an imagined landscape, naming the main geographical features and buildings. Beneath the map, write a richly detailed descriptive passage of the landscape. Make use of colours and, as Tolkien did, add information about the sky and the weather.

053

A starting point

Buried deep in *The Fellowship of the Ring* is a single sentence: 'At that moment there came a knock at the door'. It's a typical Tolkien sentence – brief, informative and clear. The reader, of whatever age, will be naturally curious about who is knocking.

Exercise: Using Tolkien's simple sentence as a starting point, write a plan for a story under the headings below. List a minimum of three characters (people or creatures). Describe where the door is (for example, in someone's house, in a tree trunk, or underground) and identify the time of day. Outline what happens, including how the episode ends.

Once you've done this, use the remaining space to incorporate these elements into a descriptive passage of 200 words.

Who are the characters?

What is the location?

When is it taking place?

What happens?

How does it end?

J. K. ROWLING

BORN: 31 July, 1965
DIED: N/A
WRITING: Fantasy adventure
KEY WORK: *Harry Potter* series

J. K. Rowling is an English author famous around the world for her ultra-successful series of Harry Potter fantasy adventure stories. The books have won numerous literary awards and broken sales records, as well as spawning a series of films.

A delayed train journey

After graduating from Exeter University, she worked in the north of England. It was while waiting at Manchester railway station for a long-delayed train to London that she got the idea for writing a story about a young boy attending a school of wizardry. She began writing the story, then taught for some time in Portugal, before moving to Edinburgh following a divorce. She arrived with her young daughter and the initial chapters of the first *Harry Potter* story. As a single mother in Edinburgh, J. K. Rowling lived on state benefits, continuing to write in local cafés, while her daughter slept in a pushchair. A grant from the Scottish Arts Council enabled her to keep writing.

In 1995 the *Harry Potter* story was finished and a literary agent agreed to act for her. The manuscript was rejected by a dozen publishers, but eventually found a home with a London publisher, Bloomsbury. The book, *Harry Potter and the Philosopher's Stone*, was published in 1997. The first edition was a mere 1000 copies, which is the usual print run for a first novel by an unknown author.

From rags to riches

By the time the fourth book, *Harry Potter and the Goblet of Fire*, was published in 2000, the series had become astonishingly popular. The fourth instalment set a record for first-day sales. Sales of the fifth book in the series, *Harry Potter and the Order of the Phoenix* (2003), smashed all existing sales records. Excited children, dressed as their favourite characters, formed long lines outside bookshops, desperate to buy copies. There was Harry Potter mania. *Harry Potter and the Deathly Hallows* (2007) completed the series of seven books.

Rowling's rise is a contemporary rags-to-riches story of extraordinary proportions.

In her Commencement Address at the Annual Meeting of the Harvard Alumni Association, J. K. Rowling focussed on the 'benefits of failure' as she outlined how a background of poverty and disappointments in her early life made her more determined to succeed as she pursued a writing career.

Fans can visit platform 9¾ at King's Cross Station, London – one of many Potter-related tourist spots.

> '*J. K. Rowling's skills as a storyteller are on a par with R. L. Stevenson, Conan Doyle and P. D. James.*'
> – **Melvyn Bragg, writing in the British newspaper** *The Observer*

In just a few years J. K. Rowling had gone from being a single mother living on state welfare to one of the wealthiest women on the planet.

A host of characters

Harry Potter, Hermione Granger and Ron Weasley are the iconic trio of children with whom the readers strongly identify. In addition, Rowling created a vivid cast of supporting characters, from loathsome Dudley Dursley to Professor Albus Dumbledore, from Rubeus Hagrid to Severus Snape. The cast list is Tolkien-like in its length. And like J. R. R. Tolkein and C. S. Lewis, Rowling has imagined other worlds that are densely detailed. Uniquely, the stories combine an old-fashioned English private boarding school with wizardry and witchcraft, horror, magical games and humor. It shouldn't work, but it does, and to terrific effect.

Given her success, J. K. Rowling's work has inevitably attracted criticism. Some have objected to what they perceive as evil black magic, and one critic said the books could have been written by a nine-year-old, so clunky and pedestrian is the prose. Against this are plenty of advocates. The author and critic A. N. Wilson said, 'There are not many writers who have J. K.'s Dickensian ability to make us turn the page – to weep [...] and a few pages later to laugh at invariably good jokes'.

What is undeniable is that Rowling (like the much-maligned Enid Blyton before her) can tell a story. The narrative moves at a tremendous pace, and the eye cannot seemingly keep up with the desire on the reader's part to know what is going to happen next. The books are page-turners par excellence.

 # 054

An introductory speech

In *Harry Potter and the Order of the Phoenix*, Professor Dumble-dore, Headmaster of Hogwarts School, gives the 'usual start-of-term notices' to the assembled students:

'First-years ought to know that the Forest is out of bounds to students [...] Mr Filch, the caretaker, has asked me, for what he tells me is the four-hundred-and-sixty-second time, to remind you all that magic is not permitted in corridors between classes [...] We are very pleased to welcome back Professor Grubbly-Plank, who will be taking Care of Magical Creatures lessons.'

The introductory speech given by school principals at the beginning of a semester will be familiar to many people. In the extract above, J. K. Rowling takes the familiar and introduces magical overtones and touches of ironic humor.

Exercise: Write your own introductory speech, keeping the tone lightly humorous. Issue some dire warnings and invent a few memorable names – the new music teacher, for example, or a pupil who climbed Vesuvius in the holidays.

055

An extract from
a biography

In *Harry Potter and the Deathly Hallows*, Rita Skeeter, another
fabulously named Rowling character, undertakes a biography
of Professor Albus Dumbledore.

Exercise: Think of a wizard's name – for example, Wizard Nastee
Spella or Wizard Plop – and write his or her biography in exactly 123
words. Sign off the piece with the biographer's name and make it
rhyme, like Rita Skeeter.

#056

A confrontation

In *Harry Potter and the Order of the Phoenix*, Harry and Hermione face a terrible danger in the enormous, repulsive shape of the giant Grawp. There is a serious confrontation. This echoes the stories of David and Goliath, and Jack and the Beanstalk.

Exercise: Decide upon, and name, two new characters. The two are on a journey and a serious danger is blocking the path. It could be a giant or some other horror. Write a piece in the third person, describing how the two overcome the danger and proceed on their way. You need to maintain until the end tension and uncertainty about the outcome.

057

Homework at a *wizard school*

Hogwarts School of Witchcraft and Wizardry, in common with all schools, sets homework. At Hogwarts, the homework will be very different from the usual run-of-the-mill subjects.

Exercise: Draw up a list of tasks intended as homework for a school specialising in magic. Name the school, and on the left-hand side of the list name the subjects (for example, 'Potions', or 'Advanced Spells'). On the right-hand side list each subjects' homework task.

Subject	Homework

Subject	Homework

R. L. STINE

BORN: 8 October, 1943
DIED: N/A
WRITING: Horror
KEY WORK: *Goosebumps* series

Robert Lawrence Stine is a prolific American author, TV producer and screenwriter who gained a reputation as 'the Stephen King of children's literature'. He specialises in speedily written horror stories.

Jokes and scares

At the age of nine, Stine found an old typewriter in the attic, took it down to his room and began typing stories and making little joke books. Rather than go outside to play, he preferred to stay in his room writing, and he has been writing ever since. As a child, he was also an avid reader of scary horror comic books with titles like *Tales from the Crypt* and *Vault of Horrors*.

He graduated from Ohio State University in 1965 and went to New York City where, under the pen name Jovial Bob Stine, he wrote jokes and humorous books for children. He and his wife formed their own publishing company, Parachute Press, and thereafter created some of Stine's most popular book series.

In 1986 Stine tried his hand at a horror story. His first teen horror novel, *Blind Date*, was an instant success. More books, with typically punchy, short titles, quickly followed, including *Beach House*, *The Babysitter* and *The Girlfriend*.

A writing machine

Stine once said, 'My job is to give kids the creeps!' His many series of horror stories quickly led to international acclaim. They included *Rotten School, Fear Street, Mostly Ghostly, The Nightmare Room* and most famously the long-running *Goosebumps* stories. Popular television programmes have resulted.

'Write every day, just a paragraph or two. Keep a journal or a diary'

– R. L. Stine, replying to a reader's request for advice

Stine has described himself as 'a very fearful child', and tells how his mother frightened him with a reading of the classic story *Pinocchio*. Stine said, 'The original *Pinocchio* story is terrifying.... He goes to sleep with his feet on the stove and burns his feet off.'

R. L. Stine with a young fan at a book-signing event in Florida in 2010.

When a series seems to run out of steam, like a fad or a fashion, it is replaced by a new one. There seems to be no limit to Stine's imagination when it comes to creating horror stories, and he has created multiple brands that have proved eminently marketable. 'I can really write anywhere I am – I'm a machine,' he announced. He has also written standalone novels, contributed stories to multiauthor series, such as *Point Horror* and *G. I. Joe*, and written his autobiography, *It Came From Ohio*, another example of Stine's jokey way with titles.

Plain yet vivid

R. L. Stine is a literary speed-merchant, claiming he can complete a book in eight days. The tone of the writing is usually boisterous, with an element of the grotesque. The language is plain yet vivid, and there is often a surprise ending. Despite the speed of production and the seemingly endless flow of material, it is interesting to note what he says about his writing method: 'I do much work before I start to write. I do complete chapter-by-chapter outlines for every book. And I make a list of all the characters – what they look like and their personalities. And I always figure out the ending before starting the book.'

The books are funny and scary. They are quick, easy reads, and no one is pretending they are going to end up as classics of children's literature. Yet they do make their mark: young readers devour them, rather like burgers. The books' fans are legion.

Stine's descriptive writing is graphic, pared down and immediate. Here's an example from *The Werewolf of Fever Swamp*: 'A gust of hot, wet air rushed in through the open door. The chirp of cicadas greeted my ears. Holding on to the door, I peered into the darkness of the back garden. Nothing.' He uses dialogue equally sparingly: '"Get up! Get up!" Emily was screaming. "It's – it's got me!" I cried in a tight, trembling voice.'

058

Book titles

R. L. Stine has a distinct way with book titles. They are often short, to the point and act as excellent doorways into the stories. 'Most of my ideas start with a title', he is reported to have said. Some examples are *Piano Lessons Can Be Murder*, *Monster Blood*, *Lost in Stinkeye Swamp*, *Dummy*, *Brain Juice*, *The Curse of the Creeping Coffin* and *Zapped in Space*. Hardly subtle, but strikingly effective!

Exercise: Write Stine-like titles for horror stories, using the following prompts:

- A deserted mansion
- A railway station at midnight
- A padlocked church
- A flooded goldmine
- An abandoned space station
- A haunted bedroom
- A computer suite in a school
- An attic containing boxes of old toys

_____

_____

_____

_____

_____

_____

_____

_____

_____

_____

Now invent titles for horror stories whose principal characters are:

- A crazy school caretaker
- An escaped convict
- A tramp
- An aeroplane pilot
- A long-lost uncle
- A weird inventor

_____

_____

_____

_____

_____

_____

_____

_____

_____

_____

_____

059

An urgent exchange

In the profile on pages 152–153, there is an example of R. L. Stine's use of dialogue. He keeps conversations tight and factual. They tell the reader what's happening, without musing or meandering.

Exercise: Create a dialogue between a girl and a boy facing something horrific or dangerous, like a blood-stained zombie, walking skeletons, a vampire, an oozing ghost or a ravenous wolf. Name the children and place them in a location or setting. Keep their dialogue short and urgent as they face the approaching danger. End the dialogue with a cliff-hanger. The reader must want to turn the page to find out what happens next.

060

Briefs

R. L. Stine uses very few words to describe settings or locations. He will often set a scene in three or four short sentences before moving on with the action and the characters' dialogue.

Exercise: Draft brief descriptions for the following scenes:

- A cave on a mountainside
- A swamp with gas bubbles breaking the surface
- A graveyard at midnight
- A disused underground tunnel

Rewrite the descriptions, keeping each one to 25 words or less.

MILDRED D. TAYLOR

BORN: 13 September, 1943
DIED: N/A
WRITING: Family saga
KEY WORK: *Roll of Thunder, Hear My Cry*

Mildred D. Taylor is an African-American author whose books explore the struggle faced by African-American families living in the Deep South of the USA. Her novel Roll of Thunder, Hear My Cry, *won the Newbery Medal in 1977.*

Difficulties in the Deep South

Born in Jackson, Mississippi, Mildred D. Taylor began her days in the American Deep South, where her life was blighted by racial discrimination. When Taylor was still a baby, her father moved north to Toledo, seeking fresh opportunity, and soon found work. Once he was established, members of his extended family followed, including the infant Mildred D. Taylor. She later said that she was 'born in a segregated city in a segregated state in a segregated America'.

In the 1950s Taylor attended integrated schools and graduated from the University of Toledo in 1965. She joined the Peace Corps, working as a teacher in Ethiopia for two years. Thereafter she settled in Los Angeles to pursue a writing career.

Family matters

Taylor's great-grandfather was the son of a white plantation owner in Alabama and a slave woman. He eventually ran away and bought a tract of land in Mississippi. Mildred D. Taylor often returned to visit the Deep South, where she heard many family stories that were at times humorous, at times tragic. She listened and drank in memories and reminiscences derived from a rich oral heritage. Growing up, she began 'to visualise all the family who had once known the land, and I felt as if I knew them too'. The strength of family ties is evident in her life, and it has become central to her writing. Her characters are often based on family members and acquaintances.

Nearly all Taylor's work centres on those oral stories she heard. She has spoken about how much history was in them, especially of slavery. Her books explore the social struggle faced by African-American families, and the importance and strength of family is a recurring theme. She created the Logan family, and they feature in her main books.

For Mildred D. Taylor, the history books she read at school misrepresented black people as she knew them. Such books had 'no black heroes and heroines... There was obviously a terrible contradiction between what the history books said and what I had learned from my family.'

Mississippi in autumn: The Deep South was a source of great inspiration for Taylor.

In 1975 she published *Song of the Trees*, in 1977 *Roll of Thunder, Hear My Cry*, and in 1992 *The Road to Memphis*. Taylor was awarded the 2003 Neustadt Prize for contributions to children's literature.

Language and character

The Logan saga is essentially a family history, and its stories are narrated by members of the Logan family. *Roll of Thunder, Hear My Cry* is the series' principal and most famous book, although chronologically it is the middle book of the series. The story follows the course of a year, and nine-year-old Cassie Logan's coming-of-age experiences. Weather is a strong feature – the book's climax features an approaching massive thunderstorm, which symbolises the violence in human affairs. In the end, rain extinguishes the climactic fire and also ends the emotional storm. Land is seen as a symbol of independence, of autonomy: a repeated refrain of a senior character is 'We won't lose the land!'

Taylor's use of language has an authentic ring: words such as share-cropping, lynching, switch (whip), welts, mercantile (country shop), gully, clapboard, chignon and carpetbagger stud the text. At first she'd used Charles Dickens and Jane Austen as models for her fiction, but she found emulating their style unnatural. Eventually found her own voice.

'When I write a story, I always hear the voices of the characters, the way they talk and how they express themselves.'

– **Mildred D. Taylor, from an interview with the American Library Association.**

Mildred D. Taylor said that her intention in writing *Roll of Thunder, Hear My Cry* was that it 'will one day be instrumental in teaching children of all colours the tremendous influence Cassie's generation had in bringing about the Civil Rights movement of the 1950s and 1960s'. The novelist herself spoke for a generation; she has become the voice of a people.

061

First day of school

In *Roll of Thunder, Hear My Cry*, the narrator, the nine-year-old Cassie Logan, recounts a walk she and her brothers took along a long dusty road in rural Mississippi in the autumn of 1933. It is the first day of school. Their mother has issued strict instructions.

Going to school on the first day of a new academic year is a rite of passage for almost everyone. It is a moment of conflicting feelings: uncertainty and excitement, nervousness and anticipation.

Exercise: Describe what you can remember from that experience. Did your mother issue any instructions or warnings? What did you notice on the way to school that day? What were your feelings?

Write the piece as through the child's eyes (in the first person).

062

Songs as starting points

Mildred D. Taylor reports that, while struggling to write her most famous book, a song came to her. It was *Roll of Thunder*. She describes how she sang it to her father and everything came through in that song. 'I told my father that day, "This book is going to win the Newbery Medal!"' And in 1977 it did.

Songs are evocative. Some people regard them as the soundtrack to their lives. Heard again, they can bring back memories of a time or a place, of an event, of being with a special person or particular people. They can bring back emotions: joy, happiness, delight or perhaps fear or sadness.

Exercise: List as many as ten song titles that, for you, have special significance. Some may come from early childhood or school days. Place them in chronological order.

For each title, write a paragraph saying where you heard the song, when, the circumstances and what it means to you. Maybe a piece of such writing will prompt you to write more, just as it did for Mildred D. Taylor.

#063 *Recalling old stories*

As a child, Mildred D. Taylor immersed herself in the stories of the past, which were related to her by family members. Those stories became of prime importance in her writing.

Exercise: Can you recall a family story you heard as a child? It may have been told by grandparents, or aunts, or uncles, or your own parents. Such stories could have been told during visits, or at birthdays, or at Christmas when the family gathered together.

Note down all you can remember about a particular story. Rewrite it, organising the narrative piece so that is has a beginning, middle and an end.

JULIA ALVAREZ

BORN: 27 March, 1950
DIED: N/A
WRITING: Social realism
KEY WORK: *Before We Were Free*

Julia Alvarez is a poet, novelist and children's author of Dominican descent who now lives in the USA. Her writing for children ranges from picture books to novels for young adults. She is a literary award-winner.

A challenging childhood

Julia Alvarez was the daughter of Dominican parents living in New York City. When she was still a baby, the family moved to the Dominican Republic, where they lived for ten years. She grew up in a time of great unrest and fear, under the dictatorship of Rafael Trujillo. It was a period of social strife, and her father became involved in political rebellion. The family was forced to flee back to the USA, where, in New York City, Julia Alvarez suffered racism in the school system as well as experiencing difficulty getting to grips with English.

From the oral tradition

As a child in the Dominican Republic, Julia Alvarez grew up with an oral tradition of storytelling. She loved such stories, but it wasn't until coming to the USA as a ten-year-old that in her mind she linked reading and writing with stories.

She completed a graduate creative writing programme at Syracuse University (1973–1975) and then worked as a teacher, all the time writing poems and stories. She yearned to be a writer, but in the late 1960s and '70s, as she pointed out, 'Latino literature

'I was particularly interested in the sons and daughters of those who had been tortured, imprisoned or murdered – kids like my cousins and my childhood playmates. So it was a composite both of doing research and of remembering family stories.'

– **Julia Alvarez**

CHILDREN'S WRITER'S NOTEBOOK

In contrast to the frightening turmoil of her childhood in the Dominican Republic and difficulties of her schooldays in New York City, Alvarez now writes 'mostly in my home in Vermont: a perfect space, very quiet, out in the country, very solitary'.

A photo taken in 1959 in the Dominican Republic, where Alvarez lived for 10 years as a young girl.

or writers were unheard of'. It wasn't until 1991, at the age of 41, that her first novel was published. *How the García Girls Lost Their Accents* was brought out by a small press with 'a wonderful editor willing to give a new voice a chance'. That book, along with *In the Time of the Butterflies* (1994) and *Yo!* (1997), established Julia Alvarez as one of the most significant Latina writers.

She has written many books for children, notably the *Tia Lola* series of stories for younger readers, and *Before We Were Free* (2002), a novel for young adults. Her work is strongly influenced by her childhood in the repressive atmosphere of the Dominican Republic in the 1950s, and also the difficulties with race and language that she experienced when arriving back in the USA. Her books focus on identity and the issues of assimilating into a culture.

Before We Were Free

Set in the Dominican Republic, *Before We Were Free*, a novel for young adults, centres around 12-year-old Anita de la Torre, and her experiences of the 1960 plot to assassinate the Republic's tyrannical dictator, Rafael Trujillo. Told in the first person, we see the tale unfolding through Anita's eyes, as she sees members of her extended family abruptly flee to the USA, witnesses her father and uncle being arrested for involvement in the assassination plot, and her subsequent time spent hiding, along with her mother, in the bedroom of a family friend. The perspective remains Anita's throughout. As the tension mounts, the narrator becomes ever more anxious. During the period of hiding, Anita keeps a journal.

Julia Alvarez has drawn deeply from her own childhood experiences. She handles the story with sensitivity, using muted language to communicate a sense of terror and in descriptions of imprisonment and torture. The author has a great eye for detail. The story could be seen as a family saga, albeit rooted firmly in reality. A reviewer called it 'a stirring work of art', and in 2004 it won the Pura Belpré Award. The award's committee described Alvarez as 'A Latino/Latina writer ... whose work best portrays and celebrates Latino cultural experience in an outstanding work of literature for children and youth'.

064

The journal

In the novel *Before We Were Free*, Anita de la Torre kept a journal while in hiding. The writing takes places in an enclosed space, cut off from the outside world. It includes mundane day-to-day and nighttime activities, occurrences, sounds and sights. Small things become important. The senses are heightened and feelings are expressed.

Exercise: Compose a four-day journal as written by, say, a ten-year-old girl who is being hidden to protect her from some kind of danger. Write an extended paragraph for each day. You need to get into the girl's mind and write from her perspective. Draw upon your own childhood memories.

065

A terrifying event

Looking again at *Before We Were Free*, the child narrator witnesses a terrifying event, when armed police break into the family home, arresting her father and other family members and dragging them away.

Exercise: Try to compose a description of a terrifying incident, in which you are present as a child. Write in the first person from the child's perspective. The incident could be when the child and friends were trapped underground, or when they witnessed a terrorist bomb explosion, or the violence that ensued when parents discovered burglars in the house after midnight.

You could experiment with stream-of-consciousness writing to achieve a sense of urgency, panic and fear. Leave out all punctuation: just let the words flow breathlessly.

#066

What to wear?

In *Before We Were Free*, preparations are underway for a family birthday party. There is an ongoing argument between Mami and teenage daughter Lucinda about what she should wear.

Exercise: Assuming the persona of a teenager, write an account of the exchanges between yourself and your mother about what is and what is not appropriate to wear at a birthday party. The trick is to make the dialogue sound authentic. Advice will be handed out and there will be impatience and disagreement, but a resolution will be found in the end.

JUDY BLUME

BORN: 12 February, 1938
DIED: N/A
WRITING: Social realism
KEY WORK: *Forever*

A prolific American author, Judy Blume has written many books for children of all ages. She is best known for her novels for young adults, in which she tackles serious and difficult subject matter.

A creative decade

July Blume reports that, for most of her childhood, she was 'making up stories inside my head', and seems to have been writing creatively ever since, producing numerous publications in the process. She graduated from New York University in 1961, and her first book, *The One in the Middle is the Green Kangaroo*, appeared in 1969. It indicated what was to become a Judy Blume trademark: an unerring ability to dream up attention-grabbing, memorable book titles! During the 1970s, she was intensely prolific, writing many of her best-known titles and gaining a worldwide readership across a wide age range. *Tales of a Fourth Grade Nothing* (1972) proved especially popular.

Frank and unflinching

In her novels for young adults, Judy Blume chose to write about young people's anxieties, concerns and worries. She spoke directly to teenagers in a frank and unflinching way, tackling racism in *Iggie's House* (1970), divorce in *It's Not the End of the World* (1972), bullying in *Blubber* (1974), masturbation in *Then Again, Maybe I Won't* (1971) and sexuality in *Forever* (1975). In one of her most famous titles, *Are You There God, It's Me, Margaret* (1970), the book centres on 12-year-old Margaret's worries about menstruation and religion.

Perhaps her own personal life – she divorced twice – and relationship experiences in the modern world fuelled her desire to explore contemporary issues, and to write candidly and from the heart. Blume received many messages from teenagers, who felt she was speaking directly to them about their private worries.

It hasn't all been plain sailing. The books have aroused concerns regarding their suitability for young readers. There has been

Judy Blume's controversial books became a target for censors, who sought to have what they regarded as sensitive material removed from bookshelves. Blume joined the National Coalition Against Censorship in order to defend intellectual freedom.

Blume meeting pupils at an elementary school in 1977. At the time she had already written 12 books.

'There are no hard and fast rules about writing, and no secret tricks, because what works for one person doesn't always work for another. Everybody is different. That's the key to the whole business of writing: your individuality.'
– Judy Blume

much controversy and Blume has been the target of hate mail. Her concerned publisher provided Blume with a bodyguard to offer protection as she travelled to and attended her many speaking engagements.

Writing for young adults is in many ways a specialist vocation. Teenagers are quick to spot artificiality and won't accept being talked down to. They might not be able to articulate their criticisms but they instinctively know when an author hasn't got it right. Judy Blume has found and honed narratives in a true and sensitive

voice, which her reading audience recognise as authentic. It is no surprise, therefore, that her stories for young adults have sold millions of copies.

Teenage love

Judy Blume's bestseller, *Forever*, attracted much criticism, due to its candid, no-holds-barred description of a teenage love affair. It became a cult hit with teenagers when it was published in 1975. Writing in the first person, Judy Blume lets the principal character, Katherine Danziger, tell the story of how she fell in love with Michael. There's plenty of 'teen' dialogue: colloquial, short, snappy, casual and with added throwaway humor. It has a totally genuine feel. The various characters in the book are wholly believable, and the story revolves around their day-by-day friendships and relationships. The sex is graphic.

In 26 breezy chapters, Judy Blume creates a world of relationships that is real. This isn't so much a work of the imagination as a picture of known and observable reality. It caused a rumpus, and the book was even banned in some markets.

067

A trusty notebook

Judy Blume once wrote:

'Before I begin to write, I fill a notebook, jotting down everything that pops into my head about my characters and story.'

Exercise: You are contemplating writing a story featuring three teenagers going for a day out at a seaside town. Compile a numbered list of everything that comes to mind about the characters, the journey, the town and what happens there.

You are drawing from your knowledge: what the characters look like, what they wear, their habits and actions, how they travel to the resort, among many other things. Do you have any experiences of seaside towns? What might happen there?

You now have a 'bank' of information upon which to draw as you write the story (500 words).

068

Dialogue exchange

Judy Blume is adept at creating characters through dialogue. She keeps conversations short and colloquial.

Exercise: Compose a dialogue between two teenage friends. One is unhappy about things that have happened at home. He or she is thinking of running away. Will the friend go with him or her? Write the dialogue as told by one of them. For example:

> Gabrielle was upset. Her eyes looked bloodshot.
> 'What's up?' I asked. 'Trouble back at the ranch? Again?'
> She shrugged. 'Maybe.'

#069

Letters

In *Forever* Judy Blume writes an entire chapter consisting of letters between a girl, who is away at camp, and her boyfriend. It is yet another literary device for telling a story and moving it forwards.

Exercise: *Forever* was published in 1975, before the advent of the Internet and emails. Compose an email exchange between a girl who is in hospital following a car accident, and her boyfriend, who has gone to stay in another town with his grandparents and is unable to visit.

The emails can be a mix of mundane happenings, gossip about mutual friends, hopes for the future and also an underlying need to express love or desire. The challenge is to create believable voices for the correspondents.

070

First meal

Getting the details right can help give a scene authenticity and help readers become immersed in your writing.

Exercise: Take a look at the following scenario:

> *It's her seventeenth birthday. Her parents are out for the evening. The new boyfriend is coming around for a meal. It's the first time she's prepared and cooked something for him. A CD is playing, the table is laid, candles are flickering and she's dressed up for the evening. The scene is set.*

Which details will really bring this scene to life? Consider the following questions:

Where have her parents gone for the evening? And do they know about the dinner date?

What has she cooked? Has she done a good job?

What music has she chosen?

How has the table been set?

In what way has the girl dressed up?

NOTES

CHILDREN'S WRITER'S NOTEBOOK

IMAGE CREDITS